Future Cities

Designing Better, Smarter, More Sustainable and Secure Cities

Edited by Dr. Joseph N. Pelton
and Dr. Indu Singh

Published by the
Intelligent Community Forum

www.intelligentcommunity.org

Contents

Preface

By Dr. Joseph N. Pelton and Dr. Indu Singh

This book is about the future. More precisely it is about the future of cities and how they ultimately shape the future of our planet. The predominant influence of cities comes from many sources. It is here that the majority of all humans live. It is here that new technologies and major scientific discoveries and inventions arise. It is here that new strategies for sustainable development, renewable energy, and combating climate change arise. Rather than trying to address all aspects of urban planning, this single book—a part of an on-going series—tries to present a coherent set of thoughts, ideas and data in a digestible-sized format that can be quickly read. Following books will seek to do the same for other topics such as Telework.

In the following pages you will read about the major forces of urban change that will ultimately reshape our world. These forces are powering the innovative transformation of cityscapes around the world; these transformations are not surprisingly characterized in different ways by different technologists, by regional urban planners or by systems and network engineers. Sometimes these new urban environments are called "Intelligent Communities". By others these new urban centers are given titles like Smart Cities, "Internet cities" or "future cities". Regardless of what these new cities are called, the concepts and the technologies they represent are reshaping the world and giving us a new view of tomorrow.

These communities—with their enhanced systems, their new technology, and their new ways of re-inventing the urban experience--will influence global evolution, spur technological advancement and redefine the human experience in the 21st century. The future city is about human potential and overcoming the challenges that face Homo Sapiens at this critical time of our evolution. We believe that the 21st century will be the most difficult and challenging century in the entire history of humankind. More people have had to find a way to live and survive on planet Earth since the start of World War 1 than in the entire history from the time that marked the start of the human race. With each decade the challenges only seem to escalate.

The Greek philosopher Alcaeus in the Sixth century B.C. expressed the centrality of the city and its future in a way that remains timeless: "Not houses finely roofed, or the stones of walls well-built, nay, nor canals and dockyards, make the city, but men able to use their opportunity."

In the pages that follow we will explore the insights of planners and systems engineers such as Ms. Christine Robinson and her colleagues at CSC who have developed new concepts in urban security for government agencies in the U.S. and abroad. We will learn from the experience of Dr. Indu Singh and his team at Deloitte, who have helped to design "smart cities of the future" and "intelligent Internet communities" on several continents around the world. Here we will examine how economic, business and services to citizens are the key drivers in the design of Intelligent Communities of the future. Also when we examine "security" in the design of the future city—we learn to think of "security" in the broader context of the word.

The interrelationship between the city, the evolution of humanity and new technology remains an incredibly powerful one. Clearly the future of cities has many dimensions related to art, culture, education, health care, business opportunity, trade, political relationships, governmental and military systems and much, much more. Nevertheless communications and information technology (IT) are incredibly powerful drivers of change and are a key focus in this book. In the United States cities such as Philadelphia are using "smart" recycling bins embedded with RFID tags to track and encourage residents for recycling. In recent months, the government of Kenya successfully designed and implemented an elaborate e-learning program. This distributed tele-learning program was able to train over 22,000 nurses in the basic medical skills necessary to treat diseases such as HIV/AIDS, malaria, and tuberculosis. In China, the world's largest electronic education program known as the Chinese National TV University, was started in 1986 as an Intelsat-based satellite experiment under Project Share. This system now provides innovative programming to over 5 million students. In Korea, transportation managers have deployed a network of wireless sensors to ensure the safety of bridges throughout the country.

These are only a few examples of how technology is redefining our world and the move toward what has be called an electronic global village. (See the recent reports from the Information Technology and Innovation Foundation (ITIF) to explore dozens of other examples of how technology is helping to define the future city. Also see: *Digital Prosperity: Understanding the Economic Benefits of the Information Technology Revolution* (2007) and *Digital Quality of Life: Understanding the Personal and Social Benefits of the Information Technology Revolution* (2008), ITIF, Washington, D.C. www.itif.org)

The pages that follow explain our vision of how Intelligent Communities are defined in many ways by technology of all types as well as innovative systems planning techniques. We do not claim that technology and innovative system planning are the only force to be considered, but this book does seek to underscore how these "drivers of the future" must be considered in any effective approach to urban planning.

Annex A to this book, for instance, records and sum-marizes a remarkable catalog of the most important human inventions. These inventions, from vaccines to nuclear power, from telescopes to computers, have transformed society in remarkable ways. We invite you to review this catalog to see what inventions we have missed and which technologies have proven to be a positive force of change and which have perhaps undermined or retarded a "better" future.

One of the unifying themes in the pages that follows is that technology not only drives important changes, but that the rate of change continues to accelerate and ever more rapidly. Let us consider a "thought experiment" to illustrate the point.

First, let us imagine a person who leaps across time and space from the age of Socrates and Plato to the time of Napoleon and Thomas Jefferson—a distance of some two thousand years. The transition would not be all that stark. The cities, the buildings, the horse-based transportation systems would seem quite familiar.

Now think about transporting a person just two hundred years forward from the start of the 19th century to today's world. Jumping from then to the contemporary world would be mind-boggling. That person certainly would not be prepared for computers, PDAs, and the Internet. They would not be prepared for a world of maglev trains, metro systems, and—gasp—even space travel. They would certainly not know what to make of artificial intelligence, robots, artificial hearts, brain surgery, prosthetic devices, and a complex world society of well over six billion people armed with nuclear weapons. They would have difficulty understanding the intricacies of global trade and finance, permanent colonies in Antarctica, and satellite systems to support instantaneous global communications, remote sensing or probes that fly beyond the reach of our Solar System.

Clearly we live in a time of awesome future compression where the world changes in a flash. The age of personal computers and the Internet is less than a quarter century old. We are constantly challenged to adapt to new, difficult and potentially dangerous new environments and risks. The depletion of the ozone layer, genetic mutation, terrorist attacks via weapons of mass destruction, climate change and financial markets that can melt down in a matter of weeks are only a few of the problems that the residents of future cities in the 21st century will need to face. We have no panacea or magical insights to share. This book does describe and interpret some key trends, analyze new ways of coping with emerging new challenges and sharing useful information about important new technologies that are emerging today. It explores what urban planners and political leaders have found that works in their communities.

We particularly salute the research that the Intelligent Community Forum has undertaken in recent years.. The ICF is providing a useful service by examining and publishing key information about what many city leaders and planners are doing to design and achieve improved communities. We hope that this book helps urban planners around the world to envision better, more secure, more responsive and more livable cities of the future.

CHAPTER 1

Cities as the Cradle of Technology

By Dr. Joseph N. Pelton

Chapter in Brief

The key to the future can often be learned by considering the wisdom of the past and by avoiding historical mistakes. This opening chapter explores how cities came to be and how urban centers that allow specialization are often the main cradle of technology. Reviewing history can help us identify key goals we need to pursue in planning for future cities. Urban planners, economists, political philosophers and behavioral scientists have all contributed to thought about creating a better future. The ideas of thinkers as diverse as Sir Thomas More to Sigmund Freud, from Jacques Ellul to B. F. Skinner are explored in considering new and improved environments that could be achieved in the 21st century.

Dr. Pelton is the award-winning author of over 25 books related to the future, applied space systems and communications networks. His books explore not only how technical systems work, but how they impact society. He is the Former Dean of the International Space University and former head of Strategic Policy at Intelsat.

"Technology and Humanity are inextricably linked" —
Buckminster Fuller

Cities that afford defense to their citizens became possible
when wild wheat, known as husked emmer, began to yield
enough seeds to make farming viable sometime around 8,000
BC. This random event, a chance mutation of vegetation,
occurred nearly 10,000 years ago and changed the course of
human history. This occurrence, which might be called the
"first green revolution," made permanent settlement and farming possible. Since that time towns and cities have evolved to
reflect the growing complexity of modern civilization. People
have found more and more ways to build cities that afford
them increased opportunity. Potable water, food, shelter and
common defense were among the first opportunities that the
first cities offered. In time, others followed. These included
education, the first elements of health care, cultural and religious practices, more sophisticated defenses and weaponry,
and the advent of tools and craftsmanship.

Ultimately the city with crowded streets, urban congestion, and growing levels of waste and garbage has also led to
or at least fostered other undesirable side products. These
include a variety of pollutants, criminal behavior, cultural,
racial and ethnic clashes, slums, traffic congestion, health concerns, vulnerabilities to natural disasters and most recently
terrorism. It will be strongly argued that the city did not cause
these side effects but nevertheless the advent of the city and
urbanization has changed how people live, work, engage in
warfare, and interact socially, economically and culturally with
their fellow human beings. Indeed the city and human presence on the planet has begun to impact the planet's very ecosystem. If the failed experiment in the Arizona desert called
Biosphere II proved anything it confirmed we do not yet know
how to sustain a human civilization and a viable long-term
biosphere in which humans can survive for the longer term.

Thus one of the great challenges of the 21st century is for humans to figure out how to design and build cities that are better, smarter, greener and more secure. In a word that has become overused and often misunderstood, we need to learn how to design a sustainable urban environment. And this must not be sustainable just for the short term. A sustainable city will require an economic system that rewards survival and intellectual growth rather than just material gain and population expansion.

As farming became more productive and seed yield increased from 8,000 BC to around 3,000 BC, the opportunity for specialized craftsmanship evolved. Stone masons, butchers, tailors, carpenters, ship builders, artisans, threshers, millers, armor and weapon designers and builders, chemists and even architects emerged as the benefits of specialization and invention became clear. The city, by about 2,500 BC, at least in China and the Middle East, became a center for learning, trade, commerce, banking, transportation, arts and culture. Cities produced innovation and ideas and new tools for defense and commerce and civilization writ large.

Indeed the city and civilized life arose within a society where technology and tools could blossom to generate new wealth and power. Prosperity came to those who lived within the protection of its literal and figurative walls. Tools, invention, culture, learning, technology and specialization have become synonymous with the city now for many millennia.

The next era in the development of the city came with the birth of the Renaissance and the international exchange of newly discovered scientific knowledge. Especially from the 17th century onward, we saw what Teihard de Chardin has called the birth of the "Noosphere". In this new era of the Noosphere, the idea of the city and civilization took on a new dimension. Human innovation and the dimensions of what might be called modern urban culture began to grow at unprecedented speeds. The rate of innovation not only accelerated, but even the rate of the rate of innovation increased. This fourth order rate of change is called by physicists "Jerk". In the physical universe this can only apply to very short-lived events such as explosions.

Technology and human economic development has thus continued to grow unabated for many centuries now and at an explosive and often uncontrolled pace. It was only in the 19th century, however, that there was a recognition that human technology, economic development and trade might ultimately lead to new types of challenges. These challenges—which have led in such directions as globalism, North-South information gaps, techno-terrorism, and global warming—now transcend the conventional notion of the city or even the nation state.

These new challenges suggest that humans may need to approach the future in new ways. As billions of homo sapiens increasingly become the dominant life form on planet Earth and start to impact the balance of the planetary biosphere in terms of methane and carbon dioxide production, alteration of the polar cap albedo, and reduction of the number of species that can survive on the planet, urban planning takes on a whole new meaning. We must consider not only human terrorism and security, but also ways to create cities that are "smart", "green", and "survivable". We must create economic incentives that can sustain life rather than simply maximize industrial throughput.

The world's first international organization was the Commission on the Rhine River Basin that was formed some two centuries ago to address the issue of rampant pollution of the river due to ink being dumped into the river by printers and other uncontrolled pollution by individuals and cities alike.

Despite this first attempt to control regional pollution, the cities and national states have largely attempted to cope with such problems on an individual basis now for centuries. Often they have sought to use technology to cure problems as they have arisen.

At the turn of the 20th century, the London City Council was trying to cope with the problem of carting away thousands of tons of horse manure that accumulated on streets every year. They, in fact, had a presentation about a new technology that would rid their streets of horse manure and rid their city of unwanted pollution and also free them of a task that was threatening to bankrupt the city treasury. The answer was the new and "clean" automobile that was seen as a technological cure to their woes.

It is thus a very ambitious and perhaps even arrogant undertaking to try to see how we humans might undertake to design the Future City that embraces the best and brightest of our 21st century technologies to build a better, brighter, greener and more secure city for centuries to come.

The Need for Integrated Thinking and New Economic Incentives

Yet that is the objective of this book. We are seeking to suggest to architects, urban planners, electrical and computer engineers, as well as those concerned with education, health care, transportation and energy planning, ecology, defense and security, that there might be a better way forward. The development of the Future City starts by learning from history and lessons from the past. The first lesson is that one must start with viable socio-economic and cultural concepts about what a Future City must accomplish. We must start by defining the strategic longer-term issues that must be faced if humanity is to long outlive the 21st century. What good is material wealth if our great grandchildren face extinction because of our short-sighted focus on material goods and simply maximizing economic throughput? The developed countries of the OECD currently price wine at $50 to $100 a gallon and refined gasoline at $4 to $7 a gallon. This is the pricing system that exists even though we can grow grapes and easily replenish our supply of wine while petroleum supplies are finitely limited. After reviewing this history, Chapter 2 examines more closely key new urban technologies that can allow future cities to be realized. Nor does the future city imply the need to create a totally new city. Much of the technology reviewed in Chapter 2 can be used to retrofit existing cities to meet the needs of the future.

Wise scholars such as Paul and Percival Goodman in Communitas, Thorstein Veblen in the *Theory of Business Enterprise* and even B. F. Skinner in *Walden Two* offer us some thought-provoking observations that help us to understand what needs to drive the design of a Future City. They suggest that we must design cities to aid the ultimate needs of citizens and build economic systems to meet the most basic needs of people such as survival and security rather than simply maximizing economic throughput. By the end of the 21st century we must be fueling intellectual, cultural and environmental growth as much as material wealth and economic consumption. At least that seems to be the needed formula if humanity is to sustain a viable ecosystem suitable for our great grandchildren to survive and strive.

That is to say that if cities are filled with modern conveniences, cheap energy, fast transportation, etc., but are not sustainable in terms of long term survival of the species then we are in BIG TROUBLE! Soon we must decide if we are going to continue the model of cities based on more and more material consumption and convenience or something different. If we are going to be able to design and build cities that can sustain us for the longer term, and also are convenient and appealing, then there is hope for the future.

In short, the first question is how to design urban systems and economic processes that work for the longer term. In this case the longer term is not a century but an eon.

Eric Burgess, the editor of a volume called "The Next Billion Years," wrote the following in the introduction to the first book that I wrote over thirty years ago in 1974.

"Thinking matter—if that is what we are—is something very new in the Earth's history. This conscious awareness of creation has evolved during the most recent tick of the geological time clock. But the future of thinking beings is restricted only by their thinking, not by material laws…Earth has an astronomical future as a habitable planet for probably some 6 billion years, enough time, indeed, for a new race of thinking creatures to evolve once again from blue-green algae if all advanced life forms become extinct (due to nuclear warfare or natural catastrophe). But the achievements that a continuously evolving species might make in 6 billion years are unimaginable. A species might need only 50 million years to colonize the whole Galaxy, for example." (Foreword, Joseph N. Pelton, *Global Communications Satellite Policy*, (1974), Lomond Systems, Mt. Airy, Md.)

Eric's lucid caution to humanity made good sense three decades ago. It makes even greater sense today. Eric Burgess explained what he saw as the dilemma that we are still far from solving three decades later:

"The human industrialized system is not survival-oriented but growth-oriented and tries to maximize yields at the expense of survival. The two goals are incompatible; unrestrained growth always results in non-survival, whereas survival demands restricted growth to support the world's growing population. Nations are frantically trying to increase chemical and calorific throughput at an unprecedented rate. Both chemicals and calories are squandered in the process, and the bio-system on which the man-made system relies is endangered." (Foreword,

Joseph N. Pelton, *Global Communications Satellite Policy*, (1974), Lomond Systems, Mt. Airy, Md.)

It is hard to determine whether to be most startled by Eric Burgess's insight into the competitive economic process and its environmental implications or by the fact that this was written a third of a century ago. It is time that we consciously start to apply human intelligence to the problem of how to sustain the human species eons into the future.

In short, this book will have failed in its mission if it simply tells us how to build "smarter" cities with greater conveniences and increased security, but does not help Homo Sapiens create a new urban environment that helps us move toward longer-term survival. Thus a humanized 21st century Future City not only has to have a surfeit of snazzy new technologies and modern conveniences that provide greater protection to its citizenry and render speedier results, but it must also help us to reduce greenhouse gases, reduce pollution and global warming, and deploy recyclable and clean energy sources. The future cities we seek to design will move ideas and information rather than people. The sustainable cities will run on economic systems that include the "value of survival and pollution control" into pricing systems that will not be conveniently discarded at the next economic downturn. The key will be to create a new "growth economy" that will be fueled by green technologies and recycling energy sources.

The Future: Utopia, Eutopia or Dystopia?

In the parlance of the Greek there were three definite views of the future. These were of a utopia (a perfect place), a eutopia (a good or better place, but not perfection) and a dystopia (a bad and undesirable place). Through the ages many authors and visionaries had made attempts to describe utopias starting most notably with *Plato's Repub*lic. These many attempts to describe utopias have typically started with a principal means to achieve this end. Plato in the Republic thought to use concepts of governance and the enlightened dictator. St. Augustine in the *City of God* used many of Plato's concepts but substituted God's religious directives for enlightened human governance. Francis Bacon and Sir Thomas More, both trained as lawyers, drew upon the rule of law. At least More was realistic: his *Erewhon* described a "utopia" whose name was "nowhere" spelled backward.

In the nineteenth century there were attempts to described utopias based on economic systems followed by twentieth century writings such as B.F. Skinner's Walden Two. These latest "utopias" attempted to invoke socio-psychological concepts of so-called behaviorism. Or alternatively we heard from the "dark side".

These writings were what might be called dystopian literature. These stories projected not a future utopia, but rather a future world of oppressive leaders employing oppressive technology. Books such as *We* (Yevgeny Zamyatin), *Brave New World* (Aldous Huxley), *A Clockwork Orange* (Anthony Burgess), *1984* (George Orwell), *Fahrenheit 451* (Ray Bradbury), and *Player Piano* (Kurt Vonnegut Jr.) projected futures that were grim, oppressive and in one way or another despoiled by technology. Indeed the world of writers about the future oftentimes seemed almost evenly divided between technological futurists who saw technology as raising us to new heights (such as R. Buckminster Fuller, etc.) and those who saw technology bringing humanity to ultimate despair (Jacques Ellul, etc.) (For more about these conflicting views as seen from both the pro and con perspective see the quite insightful book entitled *The Technological Proph*ets).

The point is that Western literature and thought is littered with "black" and "white" and "evil" and "good", while Eastern thought more frequently thinks in terms of "gray". There is now centuries of thought that suggest that the perfect society will continue to elude human thought and governance for some time to come and that somehow we will also manage to overcome human technological errors and muddle through. The absence in literature and futurist thought is in the middle ground of not a perfectly and divinely conceived world nor one of technological horror. We need new ideas in the vein of "Eutopia"—a better and improved world that is neither a "Utopia" nor a "Dystopia". One of the things that prevents us from such relativistic thinking is human fascination with how "godlike" we are. For millennia humans have bought into the idea that we are the ultimate creation of a divine being and if we try hard enough we can create the perfect world, the perfect society and hence the "perfect city" of the future. A more sensible approach is to find ways, means and technologies that can make our cities more sustainable, more livable and more socially and economically productive.

Ernst Jones in his work *The Life and Work of Sigmund Freud* (1955 - Basic Books, New York) has served to dethrone the idea that we are the divine and final work of a creative intelligence from on high. Jones suggests that humanity, which Shakespeare has described as "godlike," turn out not to be so angelic after all. Jones talks about the three blows to the human ego. Copernicus delivered the first blow to the image of humans being created by God at the Center of the Universe when he explained that the Earth revolved around the Sun rather than vice versa. It has turned out that Earthlings live on a smallish planet that revolves around a smallish sun that is merely one of many, many billions of stars in many, many millions of galaxies within a very vast universe.

The next blow—the real crusher—was that delivered by Darwin and the evolutionary biologists. Their painstaking research explained that that the Creationist view that asserts that God created a perfect man and woman fully and divinely formed as a single act was really not scientifically correct. The idea that man evolved from apes was really a very hard blow to religious believers who had a quite different view as to how humans were handcrafted by God on high. To the devout this challenged the very depths of their religious beliefs. Such deeply held ideas about human Creation--perhaps tinged with just a bit of hubris--still have not been accepted by many millions of people despite centuries of scientific evidence to the contrary. (For an interesting historical review of the conflict between "Western rationalism" versus "fundamental belief systems" that takes us up to today's terrorist attacks by al Quaeda see: Russell Shorto, *Descartes Bones: A Skeletal History of the Conflict Between Faith and Reaso*n (2008) Doubleday, New York, New York)

The third blow came from the research of Sigmund Freud and other psychologists and sociologists that explained that certain patterns of human behavior can be explained by basic urges stored in the brain that related to survival, sexual urges and primal fears and reflexes borrowed from our evolutionary forebears. These three scientific "corrections" to traditional beliefs have been hard to accept for those who wished to believe that humans were God's most perfect and intelligent creations.

There are quite possibly new blows yet to come to humans who would like to continue to see humanity as figuratively the Center of the Universe. One such blow would be what futurist and cybernetic expert Ray Kurzweil has called the "Singularity". This event would be when technologists create a truly self-aware and artificially intelligent device that can emulate or perhaps exceed human thinking skills. These "self aware machines" (SAMs) would appear to have the thinking and innovative skills of the HAL 9000 computer made famous in the Arthur C. Clarke and Stanley Kubrick film: "2001: A Space Odyssey". The broad availability of machines that could perform most services that people do today would dramatically shift the world economy. Such Self Aware Machines could take over most agricultural, mining, manufacturing and indeed professional services jobs. It is hard to think what jobs might be left for humans to do. These remarkable machines, with the proper robotic or cyborg components, might become teachers, inventors or conceivably even prostitutes and criminals or on the other end of the spectrum clergymen, policemen or soldiers.

The key to planning for the future is not to define it in a single and utopian way, but rather to envision many possible futures and test how they might lead to a better, safer and sustainable way forward. The purpose of this exploratory study can neither be characterized as unrealistically utopian nor negatively dystopian. No -- the object is to examine ways to make things that, on a step-by step, technology-by- technology basis, create a better and more viable world.

New Goals for the Future City

The fundamental questions must therefore center on what do people need for long-term survival and satisfaction. Some of these basic goals and objectives must include:

- Security and protection against threats, invasion, terrorism and crime.

- Food, water, housing, transportation, energy, and basic utilities that are safe, non-polluting, constantly recycling, affordable, and sustainable. (Here were are using Dennis Meadows' definition of sustainable in that one is not using up a resource or a capability faster than it can be replaced.)

- Economic systems that will provide at reasonable and affordable levels education, health care, quality and safe products, reasonable employment, and retirement care. The trick is that this economic system cannot be based on constant human population and industrial growth and must "price in sustainable energy and essential life-sustaining products, services and commodities". (Goal number two, in particular, suggests that our economic system need to find a better way of pricing in the "cost" of sustaining viable sources of energy, transport, water, etc.)

- Social, cultural, artistic, religious and political systems that are open, non-oppressive, intellectually stimulating, and can progress to new levels of understanding and social cohesion.

- Global systems that are sustainable, balanced and self-reinforcing rather than competitive and clearly not based on mounting levels of consumption of resources, calories and energy.

There have been various "political systems" that have been employed over time from socialism and communism on the extreme left to fascism and Nazism on the extreme right and various forms of democracy and dictatorship that have promised to deliver citizens a better life and improved economic, cultural and social systems. The most sophisticated city in the world, employing the latest in telecommunications, computer and information systems, remote sensing, and "smart energy" technologies that is not able to deliver the core values outlined above will ultimately fail. Further, social-economic-political systems that are able to deliver the above payoffs, even if they employ less sophisticated technology, must be considered successes.

The point is that technology can help, but only as an adjunct to a basic framework of agreed social goals, a viable and just legal system, and the above stated society objectives. Further technology can often help the most when some of the above values come into conflict. Today many free market economic systems are designed to bring down the cost of products and maximize profits, but do not include in their valuation such factors as pollution, survival needs, and longer term societal goals related to education, health care, renewable energy, pollution controls, etc. It is in these areas where wise deployment of technology may well help or adjust economic systems in the right direction. The wise deployment of technology to meet long-range human survival goals may be the greatest challenge of the 21st century. For a very long time, we have seen material wealth, comfort and convenience as being in conflict with clean energy and green practices. The great challenge is to see if we can develop technology that can deliver both comfort and longer term survival. One possible way forward would be to change our pricing and business systems so that ecological balance and sustainability is a part of the cost equation.

In the chapters that follow we examine not only what drives the development of effective, modern and secure cities but analyze what technologies can aid in making urban infra-structure better, faster, stronger, more effective and/or cost efficient. In particular we examine how the following specific technologies and their applications can help create a better world:

- Telecommunications systems

- Information and broadband wireless IP based networks

- Advanced smart sensors, nano, MEMS (Micro-Electronic Mechanical Systems) and bio-medical systems.

- Space systems (including communications satellites, remote sensing and space navigation systems)

The objective is not only to explain existing and emerging technologies, how they work and their costs, but more importantly to explore how they can make new applications and services possible. In particular, we will explore how these technologies can make possible better education and health care systems, better and safer transportation systems, more environmentally-friendly capabilities, new business and commercial services, and more secure urban and defense systems. Many of these technologies and applications to create better cities and living environments for civilians are closely parallel to the technologies and services that support advanced military and defense related programs. Thus the parallel nature of many of these technologies and systems will be examined in terms of comparing how they are alike and dissimilar. Further, the interactive nature of the research and implementation programs associated with these technologies will be examined to see where military programs help to advance civilian applications and vice versa.

The Importance of Digital Systems

The diverse technologies investigated in this book may seem quite wide-ranging and dissimilar but, in fact, they have much in common. Virtually all of these technologies are driven by common or at least closely parallel trends.

They are, for example, driven by digital processing techniques. Digital operations make communications, Information Technology (IT), robotics, sensor devices, remote sensing and imaging, as well as space navigation systems better and cheaper. Digital processing allows these systems to be more efficient, achieve more instructional processes per second, allow faster, more effective and denser memory storage, and also afford higher levels of reliability and system availability. Digital systems also stimulate more efficient applications and services to evolve and can enhance interoperability as well, especially as the Internet Protocol becomes the common standard for virtually all services worldwide. Common digital tools and standards can be used to provide more efficient educational and health care services, better police and fire-fighting operations, better traffic and transportation and energy-related controls, and literally thousands of other services.

The so-called Pelton Merge (See Figure 1.1 below) suggests that digital transmission and memory capabilities, digital services, and digital standards will allow more and more throughput efficiency, more market integration, and more cost-effective delivery of services in the 21st century. It will also allow diverse transmission technologies to integrate seamlessly together. This will allow the "smooth marriage" of such as technologies as fiber optic and coax cable, broadband terrestrial wireless (i.e. 3G and 4G cellphones, Wi-Fi and Wi-Max), communications satellites, power line communications systems, high altitude platform systems and any other communications or networking capabilities that may evolve over time. This vision of the future, unlike the so-called Negroponte Flip, sees wireless and wire-based communications technology, not as being in competition with one another, but an increasingly integrated whole.

Already we see that digital services have integrated together to create what has been called the new "ICE" age—where ICE stands for integrated Information, Communications and Entertainment companies (such as Microsoft and Disney). We also now see references to the 5C Industries—where the reference is to Communications, Computers, Consumer Electronics, Cable Television, and Content. When these "digitized markets" are viewed as an integrated whole they represent trillions of dollars in sales worldwide and perhaps one-tenth of all economic activity on the planet. This process of digital integration can be first traced to the fields of telecommunications and computers.

The Pelton Merge

As can be seen in Figure 1.2 below, the telephone and the computer industries and technologies started only sharing electro-mechanical characteristics, but in time, with the invention of the transistor, the integrated circuit, the Large Scale Integrated Circuit, and ultimately the monolithic device the communications and computer convergence also ineluctably occurred.

As we move onward to quantum computing it will increasingly become a world where millions of new "software defined functions" will ride on top of a host of digital processors to do whatever function the user desires.

Figure 1.1: Digital Integration of Services Via Multitude of Network Options

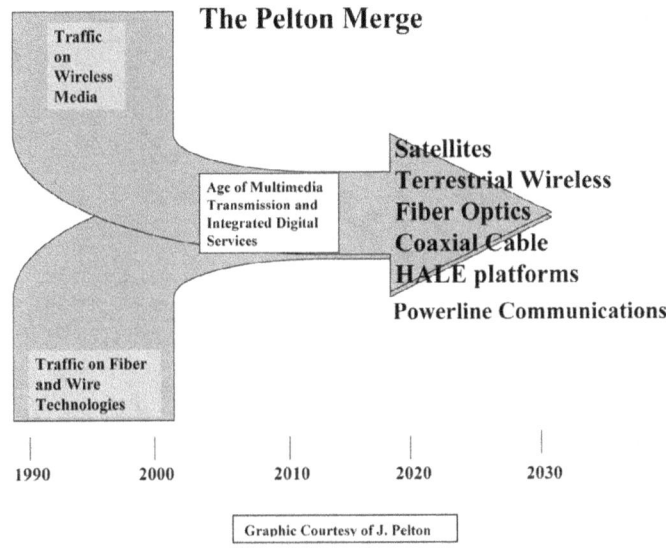

Graphic Courtesy of J. Pelton

The process started with the digital conversion of the telecommunications industry and this transition led increasingly to overlap with computer technologies. This led to the closer and closer integration of these two fields in what is now called networking. The late and former NEC Chairman Dr. Kobiyashi was perhaps the first to note in published form the merging of the fields of digital computing and digital communications. He called the phenomenon the C&C revolution. His depiction of this historical integration process is provided as Figure 1.2.

The process has continued to grow and thus the digital revolution has tended to eliminate the boundaries that have served to define traditional market sectors.

Figure 1.2: The Convergence of Communications and Computers (C&C)

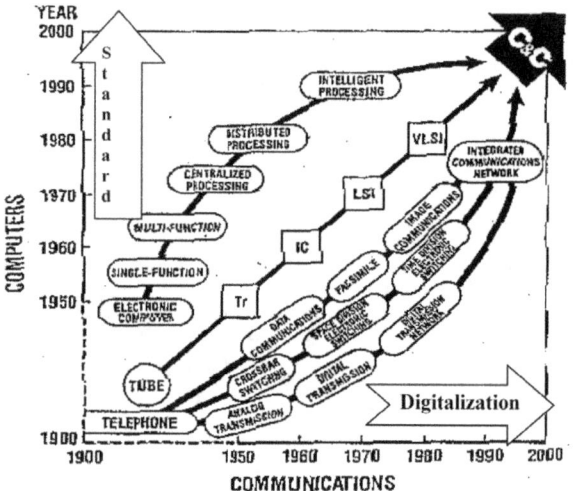

This process, called rather cataclysmically the "Big Bang," means in a practical sense that the technical and market barriers that separated various industries in the past have continued to vanish. The impact of the new digital technology on traditional market separations has now become enormous. The old technological barriers that separated parts of the news, broadcasting, entertainment, publishing, communications, computer, educational and health care industries are increasingly meaningless as new digital services and applications emerge, is shown in Figure 1.3.

It will probably take a new approach to R&D to achieve the type of breakthroughs in new technologies and operating systems that will deliver the type of future cities that we will need before the end of the 21st century. This will most likely require a new valuation system, driven by government investment and far-sighted entrepreneurs, that see the importance of what might be called survival technologies. This will likely start by recognizing a hierarchy of "survival needs" that might be loosely related to Maslov's "Hierarchy of Needs" for individuals.

Technology Implications - Obliteration of Industry Structure

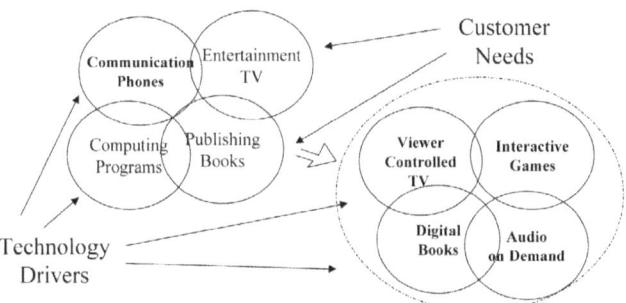

Profound technology advances and unmet customer needs will obliterate tradition industry structures and regulatory boundaries

(Graphic Courtesy of J. Pelton)

Figure 1.3

Applying Intelligence to Transportation Systems

For the purposes of illustration, let's take a straightforward case of planning for new transportation systems. This one illustration drawn from the field of transportation represents a very good example of how one can build from simple systems to more complex systems and over the longer term achieve integrated and longer range values and goals. In Figure 1.5 below we will start with examples of the least important advances and build to the most important. Although we start with the example of transportation to illustrate the concept, it is important to undertake similar integrated planning and value setting in all areas required to design a more livable and secure future city. In the following chapters, beginning with Chapter 2, we will examine how innovations across a very wide spectra of interests and services affect planning for the future. These will include innovations in security, communications, tele-work, and energy efficiency and "green technologies" that affect many design functions and goals. Thus a process of building capabilities and using more sophisticated technologies and design goals will be needed to adjust to the many challenges of the 21st century. Thus, the following chapters provide a number of insights as to how to plan for and implement the Future City.

Figure 1.5
Hierarchy of Technology Needs in Transportation

Level One	Transportation congestion detection and communications system	Adds convenience and lessens fuel consumption
	Automatic spacing of automobiles, trains or aircraft to achieve improved throughput and lessen accidents	Add safety, convenience and lessens fuel consumption
Level Two	Improved internal combustion engines or jets to achieve greater fuel efficiency (A hydrogen fueled car or aircraft could in also reduce pollution. See level three)	Significant impact on fuel consumption
	New standards for fuel efficiency or for emissions for automobiles and trucks	Significant impact on fuel consumption
Level Three	New types of clean engines and fuels that produce less pollution and heat (i.e. hydrogen, enhanced electric battery systems), etc.	Reduction in pollutants by at least 50% for each new engine.

	Vacuum Tunnels for hypersonic maglev trains	Significant reduction in jet airliner transport
Level Four	New forms of telework and virtual reality systems that provide significant substitute for travel. The Rise of Telegeography!!!	Electronic communications and visualization replaces human travel
	New types of cargo and material delivery systems (waterway delivery systems or pipeline systems)	Cargo delivery systems improved in efficiency & major reduction in pollution
Level Five	New economic and financial pricing systems that substantially increases the cost of physical travel and creates major incentives for virtual travel and telework	Major shifts and improvements in global pollution and the global warming environment
	Creation of wilderness, parks, exploration and urban zones where there can only be pedestrian or self-propelled, battery or solar-transport powered systems	Major shifts and improvements in global pollution and the global warming environment

This evolutionary approach should be used throughout the planning process for the Future City —and not just in the case of transportation. All utilities including communications, power, transportation, sanitation, as well as services such as education, health care, police, fire, emergency recovery and so on should have a scaled, longer-term plan for improved capabilities. The key is to find ways to make these improvements pay off in terms of new efficiencies so that these improvements, at least in many cases, can pay for themselves. Since labor today is the prime driver of costs, this frequently will mean automated systems that will involve people being shifted to new jobs and a good deal of job retraining.

Selected Bibliography

Articles

James Dator, "Space and Society", in Joseph N. Pelton and Angelia Bukley (editors), *To the Stars: A Twenty-first Guide to Space*, (2009) Apogee Books, Ontario, Canada (2008).

Joseph N. Pelton, "The Fast Growing Global Brain", *The Futurist,* August-Sepetember 1999, pp. 24.27.

Edward Tenner, "Searching for Dummies", *New York Times*, March 26, 2006, Op-Ed Section, Page 12.

Books

Jacob Bronowski, *The Ascent of Man* (1973) Little Brown & Co., Boston, Massachusetts.

Paul and Percival Goodman, *Communitas* (1960) Vintage Books, New York.

Joseph N. Pelton, *Global Communications Satellite Policy*, (1974), Lomond Systems, Mt. Airy, Md.)

Joseph Pelton, *Global Talk* (1981) Sijthoff and Noordhoff, Alphen aan den Rijn, Netherlands

B. F. Skinner, *Walden Two*, (2005) Hackett Publishing Co., New York

B. F. Skinner, *Beyond Freedom and Dignity*, (1973) Bantam Books, New York

Thorstein Veblen, *The Theory of Business Enterprise* (2005), Cosimo Classics, New York

Web sites

Intelligent Community Forum (ICF)
www.intelligentcommunity.org

CHAPTER 2

Using New Technology to Build Secure, Green and Intelligent Cities

By Dr. Joseph N. Pelton

Chapter in Brief

In the previous chapter we explored at a high level how the city became not only a permanent place to live but also an environment that stimulates innovation. This chapter explores in much greater detail and greater depth the incredible range of innovation that now comes from the city. It explains how these innovations, in a systematic manner, must be efficiently returned to the city to allow not only the creation of a "smart community" but one that can allow humanity to reach its potential and to survive major threats such as global warming and the depletion of the Ozone layer in the stratosphere.

Dr. Pelton is the award-winning author of over 25 books related to the future, applied space systems and communications networks. His books explore not only how technical systems work, but how they impact society. He is the Former Dean of the International Space University and former head of Strategic Policy at Intelsat.

"Truth is the Daughter of Time" — *Francis Bacon*

Not only are technology and humanity closely linked but the city is in many ways one of human civilization's greatest inventions. The challenge today is not only for the city to produce innovation, but for that innovation to be poured back into the city in a systematic way to survive challenges that technology itself can breed. Technology and the city must be cybernetically inter-related to insure not only efficiency, but a rapid response to ecology-related needs, security, educational requirements and self-sustainability.

Technology and the Urban Link

There are many ways to conceive of what a city is and what it represents for humanity—past, present and especially future. As we explored in the previous chapter the prime function of a city has been to serve as a cradle for invention. Technology and urban futures are now inextricably linked and will remain so if cities are to remain vital, sustainable and adaptable to changing societal needs. At the conceptual level you cannot have one without the other.

Today, on the order of 80% of the world population lives in major and regional cities and town of reasonable size. The city has spawned thousands of inventions from methods of warfare and defense strategies to education and health care. It is "urban creativity" (broadly defined and conceived) that gives rise to new methods of construction and new forms of transportation. In time, the "city of man" will give rise to totally unique innovations such as "self aware machines" or space elevators or islands that float on the sea. The key concept to bear in mind is that these inventions of the future will evolve much faster as the amount of societal information continues to double not once a century or even a decade but at a rate measured in months or at most a couple of years.

Networked and intellectually linked communities, universities, laboratories, scientists, engineers and planners create tomorrow's reality. If you want a mental image of the future city just think of an ever-growing "brain" that produces ideas and inventions. Our future cities will constantly be hatching the new technologies needed to address tomorrow's needs. Marshall McLuhan has conceived of a Twentieth Century metaphor known as the "Global Village". I prefer to think of the future of humanity as being that of the "global brain" or the "e-Sphere". (See J. Pelton, *The E-Sphere: The Rise of the World Wide Mind* (2000) Bridgeport, Conn.: Quorum Press.)

Many urban planners might think that creating a future city, or to use Dr. Singh's terminology the "smart city", means to design and deploy handsome new glass and steel high rises, sleek transportation systems, or intricate utility networks. To many this might seem the essence of a modern or Intelligent Community, but without creativity and continuous invention, that city will ultimately fail. Innovation and invention is the essence of a future city. Furthermore, unless this creativity is ultimately deployed for the benefit of the denizens of that future city these innovations become empty and meaningless. Without creativity, invention, scientific discovery, new economic systems and incentives to create a sustainable society, plus new cultural and artistic ideas the future city cannot survive, grow and be nourished over the long term.

Although we humans have addressed many problems of the past we now face a multitude of 21st Century challenges. These new tests to survival and future livelihood include: global warming, renewable energy, and the need for networked systems to support business, cultural and economic enterprise. We also need environmentally intelligent housing, responsive transport systems, clean air and purer water—essentially—a sustainable biosphere not only for humans but all of the Earth's flora and fauna. Our collective response to these challenges requires synoptic urban planning that is much more complex than we have ever managed to date—either in the U.S. or abroad.

As we have seen so often in the past, an invention can solve one problem but give rise to another. Coal and oil gave us cheap energy but led to pollution. High rises and elevators gave us convenient and efficient offices and housing, but also led to urban congestion.

Technology and invention most often form a one-way gate. One innovation inevitably leads us to others. Human sophistication, or at least what we call progress, lead us to a more complex civilization that requires more and more technology—and also to increased vulnerabilities. Thus the way forward involves more technology and improved security systems and the need for more integrated and thoughtful planning.

The 21st Century is a time of transition. Technology needs to be harnessed to provide environmental sustainability, genetic safety, and improved security. For centuries technology has been employed primarily to promote economic growth and sustain human population and economic growth. This is no longer a viable formula for humans to survive. Now is thus the time of the future city. We must provide humans with a new type of security and prosperity that employs "smarter technology" that produces "smarter" and sustainable results. Our new technologies must support key values that will sustain us. Thus our 21st technologies need to help us achieve:

- Environmental sustainability
- Access to vital resources, especially of water, food, and clean air
- Renewable energy
- Clean and efficient transportation
- Enhanced education and health care systems

- Security (at all levels against natural and man-made disasters and terrorism)
- Broadband communications that supports virtual presence, telework, and inter-networked global services.
- More efficient trade and distribution
- Self-aware machines and artificially intelligent help systems
- Combination of architecture with efficient utility & energy systems

Sometimes we forget the rich technological heritage that in a sense represents the history of human civilization and urban development. Annex A lists some of the most important inventions and discoveries of the last few millennium. It illustrates the wealth of this invention when considered as a collective accomplishment. When this is considered in terms of what might be called "future compression" it becomes even more awesome.

First let's imagine a "building of human history". This building that stands 20 miles or 10,000 stories tall would represent 5 million years of history since the rise of the so-called Southern Ape Man. In this symbolic building, the time since the invention of the communication satellite, computers and spandex would represent about 25 centimeters (or 10 inches) from the ceiling of the top floor. (See Figure 2.1 below).

Now look at Figure 2.2 beside it. This represents the "Building of Human Invention and Information." In this representation, some 8,000 stories of the building, in terms of new information, became available to human civilization after the end of World War II. The information produced since the invention of the Internet represents the last 6,000 stories.

Figure 2.1
Building of Human Historical Development
(10,000 stories or twenty miles high)

Computers, Robotics, Satellites, TVs (10 inches from the ceiling)

Renaissance (9999th story)

Start of Agriculture, towns and cities (9980th story)

Southern Ape Man (Hunter-Gatherers (1st story)

Further, at current rates of information formation (namely a doubling of stored and available information every 18 months) this "building of human information" would extend over 300 miles out into space or over 150,000 stories by 2020.

Figure 2.2
Building of Human Information Development
(10,000 stories or twenty miles high)

All human information acquired up to the start of Internet (up to the 4000th story)

All human information at time of invention of transistor (up to 2000th Story)

All human information up to World War II (up to 1000th story)

Annex A, at the end of this book, catalogs the numerous innovations and discoveries that have been achieved on a very broad scale over the sweep of history. Modern cities could not been achieved without many of these innovations—technical, scientific, economic, social and cultural. These top inventions of all time would not have been possible without the invention of permanent settlements, i.e. the city.

The city is, of course, about more than technical innovation. Ideas from the social, humanistic, artistic, architectural and aesthetic domain have moved human civilization forward as well. Human progress has and will continue to depend on innovations from both the right and left side of the brain. Of course in many cases, innovations from the artistic side give rise to technical innovations and vice versa. From Leonardo da Vinci onward the linkage of the art and science in human innovation has been well established.

The noted novelist Vladimir Nabokov, early in his career, carried out biological and taxonomic research at Harvard (exploring butterflies of all things). But after publishing critically acclaimed novels, he switched to teaching writing at Cornell University. He left us this profound thought that actually has guided the completion of this work: "There is no science without fancy. No art without fact." Innovation often comes from the question and not the answer. No less authority than Albert Einstein said: "Questions are the hard part". We believe that the key questions come from the humanities and the arts just as much from the science and the engineering.

The rise and expansion of the "smart city" is not something circumscribed by narrow definitions of urban planning and engineering. In brief, the future of the "city" is driven by the totality of human invention. The relevance of future urban development is tied to all fields of human endeavor from the arts and astronomy to x-rays and zoology.

As the rate of human innovation continues to accelerate in an every widening number of fields, defining and achieving the livable "smart city" will become ever more challenging.

Francis Bacon, the father of the scientific method, once said: "Truth is the daughter of time." By this he meant that more study, more research, more artistic endeavor and more humans to build on the work of those who preceded them would inevitably lead to finding more truth and knowledge. This can only mean that the greatest inventions are still to come. Sir Isaac Newton, in a more modest vein expressed his accomplishments and inventions this way: "If I have seen further, it is by standing on the shoulders of giants." Today well over 6 billion Homo Sapiens stand on the shoulders of many billions of their forebears. By 2075 the number could well exceed 10 billion and perhaps be as large as 12 billion. If it is the larger number we will have failed in many regards—not only in building a sustainable society, but in inventing a better future for our descendants.

Much imagination and innovation must ultimately arise by the late 21st Century to achieve sustainable and truly Smart Cities capable of surviving climate change, shrinking oil and pure water supplies, burgeoning global population, shrinking amounts of arable land and recoverable natural resources.

Farming and the Rise of the City

Who invented agriculture and farming? No one really knows. We do know that early humans were hunter-gatherer nomads and this was the pattern of their existence for millions of years. It was late in human development (only about 10,000 years ago or about 8,000 BC) that humans began to engage in systematic farming in such places as China and in the Middle East and North Africa. Early farming was difficult, in that when seeds were planted in ancient times, every seed planted returned only two or at the most three seeds. Early farming produced sparse returns. When droughts or other natural disasters occurred, the farmers had a difficult time surviving. But over time farming methods improved. It was in the 16th and 17th Centuries that the first "green revolution" occurred. New strains of wheat and rice and other crops were developed to produce a crop with four or more seeds for every seed planted. This was also a time of other innovations. Farmers learned to use fertilizers and improved tillage of the soil as well. Despite the onset of plagues, this was the time from which human population began to swell. It grew from about 100 million people toward today's global population of well over 6 billion people. This remarkable 60-fold increase in the number of humans on our planet could never have happened without improved farming methods.

Today agriculture has become much more sophisticated, particularly in the most economically advanced countries. In these countries there are very large agrobusinesses that are highly productive and scientific in their operation. The percentage of people that are engaged in farming in countries such as the United States, Europe, Australia, Japan and Canada is only about 2 or 3 percent of the total population. This is in contrast in the least developed countries. Here the number of people engaged in farming and forestry and mining is often in the range of 60% to 80% of the workforce or even more.

With the advent of farming and start of orchards came the need to create permanent settlements of ever increasing towns and cities. This led to the need for building supplies to construct houses, bridges, waterways, ports and other structures. One of the ways to supply these needs was to create forests that could be cut for timber. In the early days wild forests were simply cut as wood was needed, but over time, it was realized that new trees must be planted and tended to meet future needs. The dangers of forest fires and disease were recognized and systematic efforts were made to manage and control forests.

Today there are many tools that can be used to support farming and forestry. Sophisticated remote sensing satellites can be used to photograph and create "pictures" from infrared sensors to detect disease, locate forest fires and even help farmers engage in so-called "smart farming". In the case of "smart farming" the images from satellites can tell farmers exactly how much water and fertilizer or weed killer or other chemicals to release for every part of their farm to produce healthy and abundant crops. These systems are now so accurate that micro-controls can maintain the supply of water and chemicals for very large farms, not in terms of square miles or hectares but in terms of square yards or square meters.

Along the way many scientists and genetics engineers have helped to make agriculture and forestry more productive. The Austrian Monk Gregor Mendel (1822-84) discovered the way to combine the best traits of plants through hybridization and genetic engineering. American horticulturist, Luther Burbank, (1849-1926) developed many new hybrids of plants and George Washington Carver, of Afro-American descent, (1864-1943) explored what types of plant grew best in what types of soils and developed a large number of new products that could be derived from agricultural products such as peanuts that revitalized the soil, but had been previously considered of low value. Without farming and forestry, modern society would simply not exist because this technology led to the town and city. This in turn led to the creation of new arts, crafts, science and inventions, that generated modern ways of life as we know it today.

Transport and the Growth of the City

The first stage in the growth of towns and cities was farming, but transportation and distribution were key to the second stage. Up until the 13th Century towns and cities were "pedestrian oriented." In the 13th century, Beijing (Peking) was the world's largest metropolis but anyone could walk the extremes of the city in a few hours and horses and ox carts could handle the distribution of goods and services.

From this period on, the growth of canals, ever more sophisticated ocean and river vessels, astrolabes and compasses allowed the expansion of cities. Then steam and combustion engines to power rail, trucking, automobiles and ultimately aviation systems drove the expansion of agricultural, mining, distribution and national, regional and urban transportation systems.

The relation of transportation systems to the growth of cities (not only for people, but for goods, services, and utilities) is enormously powerful. Without modern transportation systems, modern megacities could not sustain themselves. Food would not be there for people to eat. Workers could not get to their offices. Gasoline would not be available to fuel cars, trucks and buses. Furniture and building supplies and elevators for housing and offices would not be available or would be unduly expensive. Construction of water, sewerage, electrical and gas systems would become increasingly difficult to deploy and successfully operate. Newspapers, mail, delivery services, and dozens of activities that are taken for granted simply would no longer be available, be incredibly expensive, or be very difficult to implement.

The lifeblood of today's major cities is within their streets and freeways, rail systems, airports, waterways and canals, and utility systems. Without these essential transportation and distribution systems, cities like Beijing,

London, Paris, Mexico City, Tokyo, Sydney, Buenos Aires, Montreal, Rio de Janeiro, Cairo, and Johannesburg could not and would not be able to continue to exist. Figure 2.3 below shows the historical growth of cities over time and the increasingly symbiotic relationship between cities and transport systems.

Figure 2.3
Growth of the City

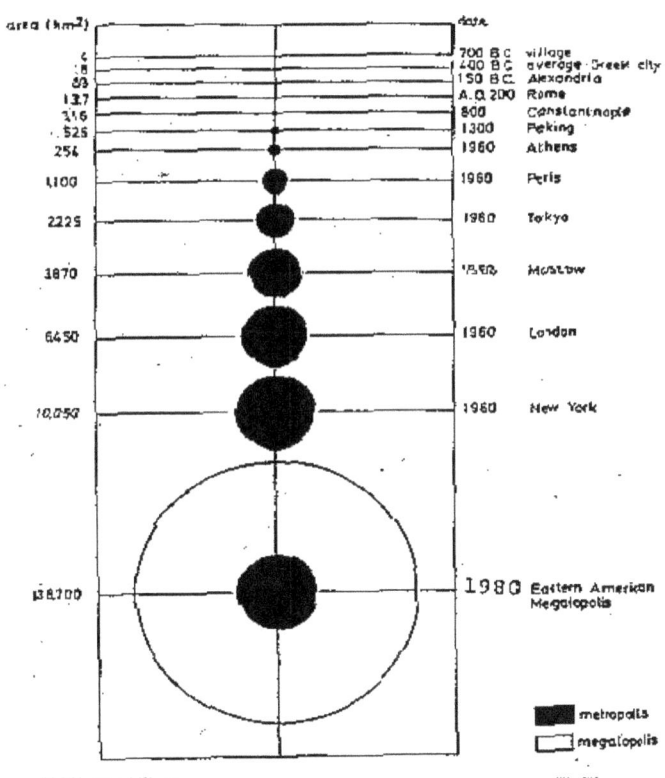

Evolution of the size of human settlements.
Source: Constantinos A. Doxiadis, "Cities of the Future" in Arthur B. Bronwell (ed.), Science and Technology in the World of the Future (New York: Wiley Interscience, 1970)

The Smart City of the Future: Drawing on a Wide Palette of Arts and Science

The first and second waves of development of towns and cities were driven by farming and then transportation. Broadband communications networks are, however, powering the third wave of urban evolution. In the age of telework and electronic banking it seems as if Internet services are gradually replacing mail, newspapers, conventional magazine and many forms of marketing. Broadband and mobile services are increasingly supplementing and even substituting for transportation systems. This revolution is just getting started but is gathering steam. Figure 2.4 lists only some of the many applications now possible with hundreds more still to come. The key to designing future cities is not to include all of these applications but to create the intellectual, telecommunications, and IT infrastructure that will allow their inclusion over time. Think flexibility, re-configurability, and sustainability.

Figure 2.4

Urban Applications and Services Via Broadband

- Virtual presence systems for Telecommuting-Teleworking
- Remote monitoring of elevator systems
- Instantaneous position location for trucks, buses, rail, ships, police & fire vehicles
- Security monitoring systems for buildings, public transit, elevators, etc.
- Remote utility meter reading and household electric power peak load reduction
- Traffic light timing adjustment during commuting hours
- Call forwarding
- Inventory control and updating
- Shipping tracking

- Tele-education and remote training services
- Tele-health services
- Emergency announcements, warnings, and evacuation measures
- On-line sales and marketing
- Smart farming using remote sensing and "remote" irrigation controls
- Remote sensing to support natural resource location, fish school location
- Meteorological observation and storm-hurricane monitoring
- Climate change measurement and tsunami alert systems
- Electronic banking, financial and insurance services
- Monitoring of urban growth, air and water pollution
- Networking of remote sensors in high rises to detect structure problems
- Networking of robotic manufacturing systems or hazardous material controls
- Automated controls for HVAC systems in high-rise with disaster over ride systems
- Continuous 24/7 business operations
- Automated systems for aircraft monitoring and take-off and landing systems

The rise of the Intelligent Community, the smart city, telecity or future city will depend on many factors. These include creative architecture, security consciousness, an emphasis on tele-services, and environmental sustainability. But perhaps most of all it will involve a new mentality that goes beyond a 19th and 20th Century high-rise mentality.

Architects such as Paolo Solari, Kenzo Tange and others in the 1960s and 1970s have suggested that urban super-density concepts known as "arcology". These brilliant architects advocated the building of megastructures to address a world of exploding population but these concepts are ultimately wrong for humanity—politically, environmentally, socially and economically.

In an age of global warming and terrorist attacks, we need to start thinking differently. We need to think in terms of distributed systems, telework, and truly sustainable environments. We also need to re-gear our economic systems to value the survival of the species over near-term growth and profits. Longer-term thinking will pay off handsomely if we allow the preservation of a humane and sustainable environment to guide our thinking.

Currently there seems to be a worldwide race to the sky. The Burdj Tower in Dubai will soon be the world's tallest building. Like Taipei 101, the Sears Tower, and other structures in Kuala Lumpur, Shanghai, etc. this structure is truly impressive. These structures represent architectural masterpieces, but intellectually—for 21st century needs—they are also a dead end. We do not need to amass huge numbers of people together via environmentally unhealthy and unproductive daily commutes that also create enormous hazards in terms of fires, earthquakes, or terrorist attacks. Distributed broadband systems can achieve high levels of connectivity via virtual presence and IT technology. Such "electronic integration" can save time and energy while achieving environmental and productivity pay offs.

Instead of more projects like Taipei 101, the Burdj Tower or the ill-fated World Trade Center Towers in New York, we need to think about architecture that can better sustain human life and the global environment as set forth in Figure 2.6 below.

Figure 2.6
New Urban Planning Priorities

Local Objectives

- Adopt "telework targets" for local government to achieve participation by at least 20% of the work force. Even police forces and fire fighting personnel can achieve these figures because of administrative support requirements.
- Create incentives for private work force to achieve similar "telework targets"
- Adapt offices to "telework" patterns so that occupied space and associated heating, lighting and air conditioning are reduced as appropriate.
- Work to redistribute workforce so that it is less vulnerable to disasters or terrorist attack

- Create opportunities for people to interact socially (in person or "on-line electronic teas")
- Explore longer range targets as the above goals are met.

State, Province and National Objectives

- Adopt "telework targets" for state or national governments to achieve participation by at least 20% of the work force.
- Create national incentives for private sector work force.
- Integrate telework objectives into environmental, energy, transportation, land use legislations with 5, 10, 15 and 20 year target goals
- Establish goals to for "cleaner" IT and telecom equipment and paperwork reduction.
- Create database to compare state, provincial and national standards

International Goals and Objectives

- Create international goals for telework among OECD countries and develop treaty-based goals to provide progress in all the areas being pursued as local, state and national level
- Create a global data base that reports on various tele-geography programs that allows easy access to comparative information in categories such as demographics, transportation, energy consumption, pollution reduction, housing and land use.
- Create international prizes for the countries achieving the best progress against objectives and the most inventive use of tele-geography in various key areas (equivalent to Nobel Prize in prestige)

Education and Training

- Develop new college, university and educational programs around the world that creates multi-disciplinary and systems planning programs to address complex problems such as transportation, energy efficiency, pollution reduction, housing and land use,

- Create study and research centers to investigate not only tele-geography, telework and integrated systems analysis and planning but also economic and pricing systems designed to reward sustainability and other practices needed to sustain humans, wildlife, rain forests, wetlands, agricultural systems, clean energy, and non-renewable resources or to create tax or other penalties to discourage practices that threaten human, wildlife and agricultural eco-system that sustains life.

- Create new study centers to examine new technologies to sustain human life, create clean energy, clean transportation systems, and sustainable living, recreation and work units.

The Longer Term Future

Broadband IT systems, environmental sustainability, recycling, renewable energy, and so on are certainly not a panacea that represents the longer-term "answer". No, technology—the thing that humans do—will continue to evolve. We will see in future decades and centuries new abilities and technical evolution. This may include self-aware machines and "smart robots", space elevators and floating islands on which all resources are recycled and all energy self generated. Indeed we should set forth challenges to create a better future. An ocean-based city that is clean and self-regenerating could not only be an interesting technical test of our ingenuity but could perhaps become a model for our future cities on the land, in the arctic regions or even in outer space.

The objective of the future city is thus not a static goal that once achieved can allow us to rest on our laurels. No—the future city is a state of mind. It is critical to understand that the only way that humans can survive is to constantly go forward to invent not only better and smarter technology but new types of artistic and cultural endeavor, new levels of understanding of the universe, and new systems that better allow us to subsist with nature. In another decade or two, it might be interesting to compare the world's greatest inventions (as listed in Annex A) to the innovations of tomorrow. This exercise would be useful to see how quickly and dramatically technology has evolved and what new wonders we have added to the list. But it would also be important to undertake in order to see how new technology had, in fact, led to new environmental dangers or unforeseen urban difficulties. A self-sustaining city that is able to generate its own energy and recycle its resources and re-purify its own water could be one of the more important of these achievements.

Selected Bibliography

Books

Joseph N. Pelton, *E-Sphere: The Rise of the World-Wide Mind*, (2000) Bridgeport, Conn.: Quorum Press.

Articles

Joseph N. Pelton, "The Rise of Telecities" in *Thinking Creatively in Turbulent Times* (ed). Howard Didsbury, Jr., (2004) World Future Society, Bestheda, Maryland, p. 117-126.

Joseph N. Pelton, "The Rise of Telecities: Decentralizing the Global Society," *The Futurist*, January-February, 2004, pp 28-33.

CHAPTER 3
Designing and Implementing Smart Cities
By Dr. Indu B. Singh with Vic Chauhan, James Gillen, Tony Hussain and Jeremy Terr

Chapter in Brief

This chapter describes key functional and planning elements required, over time, to implement what might be called a "Smart City". A Smart City is one that ultimately delivers enhanced public services, a better environment, business and job growth, expanded foreign investment and public safety. Successful Smart City implementation,—that can also be referred to as a future city or Intelligent Community, requires both a well thought out business model and public-private sector partnership. Contemporary efforts to evolve toward the first stages of a Smart City have sometimes been referred to as the "Internet city". Examples from around the world are provided of today's Internet cities. Such communities have used Information Technology (IT) systems and effective socio-economic planning to deliver better services to its citizenry and businesses.

Dr. Indu Singh is a Director of Deloitte Consulting and former Managing Director of the Bearing Point Corporation. He and his team, who are co-authors of this chapter, have extensive experience in designing and implementing Smart Cities around the world.

Cities around the world are in the midst of transformation. Many cities have embarked on new modernization plans using Smart City concepts to forge social and economic development. The consistent goal of communities around the world has been to seek to offer their citizens a modern, enhanced lifestyle. City States such as Singapore and Dubai have had early starts in such a direction. Each, in its own way, is committed to building a "Global City" for the 21st century. Others such as Kuala Lumpur in Malaysia, Seoul in South Korea and the City of Edinburgh in Scotland, to name but a few, are re-examining their next stage of growth and development to achieve similar goals. Key to all of these cities and their development plans has been their commitment to design and implement advanced new information infrastructure.

All of these "intelligent" and future-oriented cities have at least one theme in common: They have developed an integrated vision of the Smart City or Intelligent Community geared to the needs of their citizenry and business enterprises. However, the techno-economic models utilized by these various cities can be, and in fact are, markedly different. This is simply because each community has its own individual needs and culture. The move toward planning and realizing Smart Cities continues to expand and will ultimately become a global concept. Recently, countries like Saudi Arabia and the United Arab Emirates, fueled by petro dollars and also driven by a need to create a sustainable development model, have embraced a move to create a number of new Smart Cities. The advent of Smart Cities built around new broadband IT infrastructure, but also embracing other "intelligent" concepts are becoming an ever-increasing reality in the 21st century. Thus Smart Cities or Intelligent Communities also tend to include tele-education and tele-health concepts, green technologies and smart energy systems, user-friendly transportation systems and sustainable environmental and economic concepts.

Smart Cities are being created to meet new global challenges in terms of environmental protection, employment opportunities for the younger generation, and security for citizens against global terrorism and crime.

With the advent of major "global cities" in leading economies of the world, we will find new models to be examined and emulated as we also move toward an inter-networked society sometimes referred to as the "global village." Although each Smart City or Intelligent Community will be unique and different in its design and capabilities it will also have common characteristics such as:

1. Interconnected homes, work places and public institutions to enable and encourage socio-economic opportunity;

2. Increased means to help bridge the gap between information rich and information poor;

3. A "plugged in" citizenry where knowledge is shared by the various communities of interest involving all segments of society;

4. New and diversified opportunities for the younger generation; and

5. IT systems and utilities that allow cities to be more secure and prosperous.

A dynamic Smart City model that has been proven in many locales and under different forms of governance is one that is based on a dynamic and innovative public-private sector partnership. Such a model allows the private sector and "city partners" to enjoy entrepreneurial freedom, and create a vibrant city where socio-economic development and private enterprise becomes the engine of growth and prosperity.

The Smart City as a Longer-Term Planning Concept

A Smart City or Intelligent Community may mean different things to different people. However, implementation of a Smart City usually has several elements in common. One key element is the creation of a modernized city that is significantly more based on advanced information and communication infrastructure. It also encourages and employs a host of new applications to create prosperity, distribute opportunity, and enhance quality of life for citizens. The Smart City is a "citizen-centric" concept that builds on existing culture and helps forge socio-economic development.

There are several strategic and service performance advantages to such a model of the Smart City as shown below in Figure 3.1.

Since all Smart Cities have their differences and diversity is encouraged, it might be useful to examine what a Smart City does not mean:

- It is not a technology concept. It is a socio- economic development concept.

- It is not necessarily a long-term project. It is often a series of shorter-term projects carried out with long-term vision.

- It is not a single sector concept. It is a multi dimensional, multi-sector concept.

- It is not infrastructure-driven but it is service-driven.

- It is not a local phenomenon. It is a global movement with striking results throughout the world and is often a means to an end to enhance education, health care, renewable energy, prosperity, new job opportunity, and a sustainable economy.

- Success of a Smart City project is not determined by technology or capital—although these elements are important. Success is dependent on vision, leadership, and inter-group coordination.

Figure 1.3

In short, a Smart City is a fully integrated approach for socio-economic development where government, business and people are linked through a comprehensive, advanced, intelligent information infrastructure. SMART is an acronym that includes the following key elements needed to plan and implement a Smart City program. It is critical for the public, the business community and the government to team up to achieve desired goals and objectives as illustrated in Figure 3.2 below.

GETTING SMART

- Specific objectives and components,
- Measurable results,
- Agreed to by all stakeholders,
- Realistic, and
- Time framed by project's deadlines

As shown below, the Smart City is a fully integrated approach to socio-economic development where government, business and people are not only linked electronically to a comprehensive advanced information infrastructure but also linked by a common plan with realistic and measurable results.

SMART CITY 2020: Conceptual View

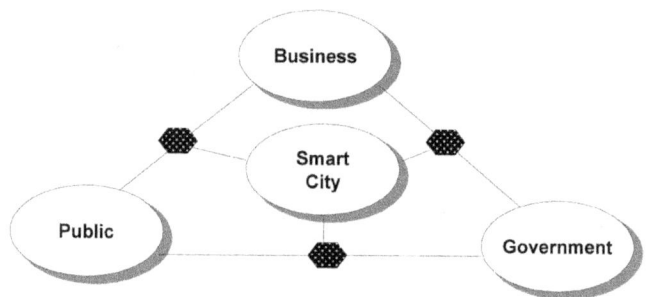

**A New Partnership Concept Forged Through the
Electronic Linkage of Business, Government and Citizens**

Smart City development requires active participation by key stakeholders including the public. The plan should seek to establish new business and trade opportunities, improved education and healthcare services, and increased capability to meet and exceed public service demand. Through information movement as well as processing and management, government organizations within the Smart City are better able to address public issues such as Green City, energy conservation, crime and terrorism prevention and control, preservation of culture and access to critical natural resources. More specifically, Smart City contributes to the following:

1. Evolution of a comprehensive local information infrastructure capable of providing global competitive advantage at the local, regional and national level;

2. Establishment of new partnerships among government, business and citizens;

3. Creation of a "model city" for further urban development through the use of information and communication technology;

4. Optimum linkage between emerging technologies and economically and socially justifiable applications and services;

5. Awareness among the user community on the potential and positive impact of technology in the business, professional and consumer sectors;

6. Ubiquitous linkage for communities as well as public and private institutions to the national and global information infrastructure;

7. Establishment of "secured city" and intelligent infrastructure thus making the city attractive for citizens, visitors and foreign investors.

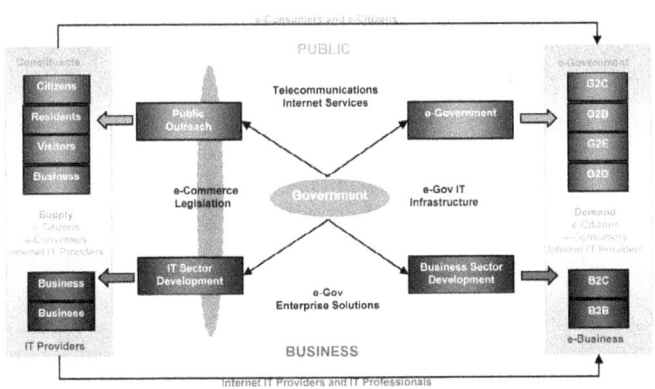

Figure 3.3: A Generic Charting of a Smart City

If planned and executed well, the Smart City can deliver market leadership, distributed opportunity, enhanced public services, a secure environment, and increased profitability.

Another way to understand the full scope of the Smart City concept is to examine what might be called the "smart city ecosystem (SCE)" as shown below. This ecosystem depicts interrelations between people, process and technology. The SCE defines the critical role of information and communication systems, and helps achieve measurable outcome of specific investments.

Creating A Smart City Vision and Strategy

The Smart City concept is an evolutionary model that puts local government, businesses and individuals at the forefront of socio-economic expansion, as well as regional and global market leadership. This process forges partnerships among citizens, public, and private institutions to transform communities into urban centers of high productivity, educational and employment opportunities, and technological advancement. Development of local information infrastructure is critical to achieving this objective.

Commencement of planning begins with the formulation of each city's vision of the future that is constructed by the community with deep roots in the local socio-cultural environment. Often, people believe that successful planning for a Smart City begins with technology implementation. Unless the foundation is built on its socio-cultural traditions and economic dynamics, however, such projects are often doomed to failure. Technology is simply the means to achieve the Smart City objectives. The technological vision should be closely linked with local socio-political and economic dynamics in close cooperation with key stakeholders.

A realistic Smart City vision is pivotal for successful implementation of what might be called "intelligent" services. The common vision is the thread that interconnects people, process and technology for socio-economic progress. Formulation of the vision dictates how information and communication technology will be used to achieve the specific objectives that are agreed.

Socio-economic and technological transformation often lie at the heart of the common vision. Vision formulation should consider the following questions:

- Where do you start?

- How do you build the partnership to develop a "win-win" strategy?

- What are the critical local and regional strategic issues and competitive benchmarks?

- What are the critical business and social needs of the user community?

- What technology and platform ought to drive the implementation?

- What is the best techno-economic model to be used?

- What is the preliminary business and social elements of the vision?

- To what extent can Smart City initiatives improve positioning in the regional, national, and global markets?

And most important...

- Given the new emerging competitive global economy and market, what is the longer-tem impact on a community if we ignore the opportunities that creating a Smart City can bring ?

Smart City Building Blocks

Cities today are presented with multiple options for developing advanced communication and information infrastructure in partnership with the private sector. Selecting an appropriate technological model is key to successful implementation of the Smart City. Third and Fourth Generation wireless technologies are driving network decisions for many implementation plans today. Although wireless networks still present a serious

The Critical Challenge: Identifying the Appropriate Mix of Building Blocks to Support the Smart City Initiative

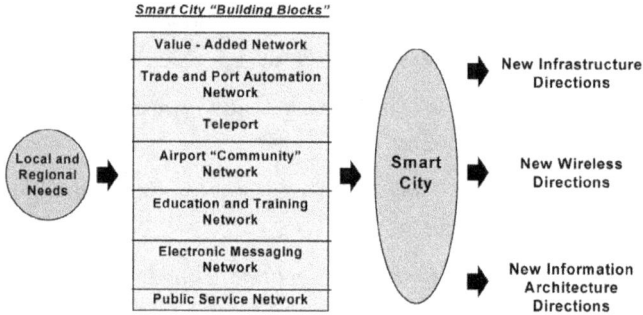

Figure 3.4 Implementing IT Infrastructure and
Software to Meet Service Needs

challenge in terms of information security, the economies of scale and ease of implementation make such technology very attractive—particularly when retrofitting a city's infrastructure. Additionally, many cities around the globe, in partnership with industry, have already laid ample fiber optics to support desired new broadband network services. These two technological developments are becoming the corner stone for the IT infrastructure of many cities. In a number of cases broadband satellite networking can become an essential third ingredient. Smart city information and communication infrastructure requires the appropriate mix of technology and systems as depicted below in Figure 3.4:

In the 21st Century, public security has taken a front seat for city governments around the world. An important aspect of Smart City planning is to provide enhanced security to citizens and visitors. Smart City supports the following:

- **Advisory System:** involves the continuous surveillance, assessment, and reporting of security threats.

- **Critical Infrastructure:** involves the security and protection of the infrastructure (e.g., transportation, telecommunications, power, cyberspace, etc.)

- **Home and Community:** involves the protection of elderly, children and their schools.

- **Banking and Finance: involves** the protection and security of our financial institutions against crimes that include bank fraud, debit and credit card fraud, telecommunications and computer crimes, fraudulent identification, fraudulent government securities, and electronic fund transfer fraud, identity theft, and counterfeiting.

- **Health and Safety:** involves the protection and security against diseases, pandemics, and bio-terrorism.

- **Law Enforcement:** involves the coordination of various law enforcement entities for enforcing the law (e.g., customs, immigration, drug interdiction, etc.).

- **First Responders:** involves the coordination of various first-responder entities when an actual emergency occurs.

In the current insecure global environment a new vision must be mapped out in terms of counter-terrorism and the protection of critical infrastructure. Modern information and communication technologies are key partners in this quest for public safety and asset protection and these strengths are addressed further in the next chapter.

In addition to information and communication technology, human capital development is a critical building block for successful implementation of the Smart City. The user community must not only adapt to technological advancements but be trained to realize their potential.

The following considerations apply to both private and public sector stakeholders in terms of recruiting and using talent to best effect:

- **Talent Acquisition:** This involves building a pipeline of skills and abilities. Businesses need to hire the necessary new talent so they can compete and grow in the new economy. This includes such things as creating strategic relationships with technical and community colleges, research institutes, and universities to ensure qualified applicants for new job openings.

- **Talent Development:** This involves recognizing and rewarding employees for innovative and creative behavior—both internal and external to the business. There could be rewards, for instance, for developing new business plans incorporating "smart city technologies", creation of Wiki groups, etc.

- **Talent Engagement:** This involves designing new knowledge management systems, cultivating a positive work environment and formalizing retention strategy to transform organizational culture.

The key to success is developing a "holistic" or what Information Technology (IT) experts call a "systems" approach to developing and implementing an overall plan. This in turn requires engaging a broad spectrum of stakeholders. It is critical for these stakeholders to buy-in, support and develop the vision. Successful implementation requires that all stakeholders in the community are not only actively engaged, but convinced in their embrace of the vision, goal and timeline. Building stakeholder engagement is key to ensuring the community develops the necessary enablers to retool the workforce, advance standards of education, and broaden knowledge and awareness of the greater community.

Where once agrarian communities were transformed by the technological revolution, great socio-economic gains can be achieved by mobilizing a workforce trained and able to employ the benefits of the broadband economy. Investments in school technologies, such as digital libraries and distance learning, can be important implementation strategies. Most successful Smart City projects have leveraged broadband connectivity to bring interactive learning into the classroom and the workplace.

As illustrated below, 70% of major change efforts within industrial sectors—such as mergers and acquisitions, downsizing or "right" sizing, and ERP—fail to achieve targeted benefits. The single largest contributing factor to such failures is people related. (See illustration below)

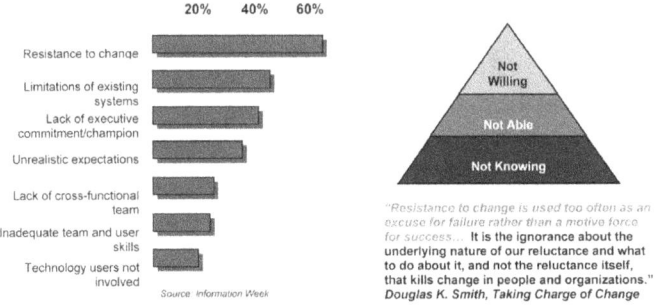

The transformational change from the conventional 20th Century city to a 21st Century Smart City is about achieving tangible, concrete socio-economic results that benefit the city's residents. Successful transformation requires organizations involved to proactively manage change and effectively leverage opportunities and even risks. Effective risk management lies at the foundation of every good change approach.

The 2007 Top Seven Intelligent Communities cited a number of innovations. One of these changes was that recently introduced in Dundee, Scotland. Here the city management replaced 10 separate card-related services in the city and integrated these into the Dundee Discovery Card. Now citizens can use the card for everything from bus service and parking to social services. This card instantly became wildly popular. The card has now been issued to 87% of 12-18 year olds for school meals and bus travel, and 85% of +60 year olds for leisure access and bus travel. The innovations can be large or small. One can use RFID to track recycled materials, use wireless and satellite networks to train a new cadre of nurses or install sensors to measure the safety of bridges and overpasses. The key is to apply the technology to meet unmet social and economic needs. The core is applying IT, telecommunications, navigation, artificial intelligence and other capabilities to improving lives. There are creative research projects currently taking place at the Media Lab at MIT designed to further this philosophy by offering new and innovative ways to redefine city transport and daily commuting. Media Lab has, for instance, devised plans for a "City Car" prototype, designed "intelligent roads", and even "intelligent parking". The MIT researchers are even exploring "intelligent" paving of roadways that include intelligent sensors.

Delivering these numerous and disparate benefits to stakeholders is critical to the success of Smart City implementation. The success will come only when there is recognition that the key is always people first. The essence of an Intelligent Community is a citizen-centric initiative built on robust enabling technology.

Smart City Models and Architecture

This model is built around the idea of focusing on specific and concrete near- term objectives while aiming at a long-term "future view" of the role of technology in the evolution of the Smart City. With the advent of an integrated Internet and mobile communication devices, the citizens of the Smart City as well as business and government communities will have multiple means to communicate within and outside the city and country.

There is power in the integration of multiple communication channels – web, fax, mobile phone, mobile computing, GIS, in-person and spatially enabled citizen relation systems. These web-like systems will extend the capabilities of a multi-channel approach in creating a user-friendly and responsive Smart City. A multi-channel approach can improve the communication between citizens and the city as well as local and national government. It can also draw global business and local new businesses into the community, and show that the city is a friendly environment for both citizens and business, promote civic pride, and provide other benefits such as stimulating new capital investment.

Tools such as standard relational database management systems can be used to efficiently store, access, manage and manipulate geographic information. This integrated approach for example, can provide a common framework, data sharing and improved decision making between the Citizen Relationship System (resident and business information) and the GIS (geographic information system).

Implementation of Smart City vision begins with the creation of business and technical models as described below:

Business Model

The first task for the implementation team should be the development of the necessary Businesses Model. This would typically consists of:

- Smart City Vision and Strategy
- Business Architecture
- Solutions Architecture
- Service Architecture
- Technical Architecture
- Performance Architecture

Smart City Vision and Strategy

The economic development concept is where one needs to start. The technology then must follow the economic and financial needs. The Assessment and Development Strategy provides a framework that provides a catalyst for development through economic transformation, e-government initiatives, and new network construction. Through targeted interventions, the city is able to provide effective and modern education as well as training and development to the workforce. A well-trained work force is needed to perform knowledge work in an effective, timely and responsive manner.

Business Architecture

The Business Architecture reference model framework represents a set of tools that enables the city and adjoining area to improve its offering and become a magnet for investment and hopefully an engine for economic growth. The Business Architecture identifies the people, processes and technology required to build a readily available, load-balanced set of business solutions. These business solutions must be flexible and adaptable to a global digital economy. The Business

Architecture must consider and include the following activities:

- *Current State Assessment* – This involves a review of current business profiles plus a review of business strategies now in place. It also includes a thorough review and analysis of current information technology architecture, organization and processes. This review and assessment provides the foundation for the design, development and implementation of new business solutions.

- *Future Model and Gap Analysis* – This part of the review and assessment identifies opportunities from the Business Model and relevant external sources. The challenge is then to develop a future Business model to support the desired future vision and analyzes the gaps between the future and current models.

- *Implementation Planning* – This then leads to implementation planning that creates a prioritized project portfolio. The plan needs to define a strategy for implementing what can be called the "must have" and "quick win" projects. The implementation plan includes project abstracts that describe the project and its benefits. In addition, the project abstracts provide the incremental costs, expected savings and expected net savings in projected reasonable range of economic gain for each project.

- *Business Case Development* – The business case then next presents the financial justification for the recommended solution. The business case should lay out the results of the above painstaking collection of data and detailed analysis in order to make informed decisions. Once the business case is clearly defined it also allows the detailed design and implementation of the proposed solutions. Thus the developing business case requires careful estimates of expected costs, the overall schedule, new revenues, paybacks, and organizational impacts for each of the implementation projects

Solutions Architecture

This Architecture provides the broad framework of the overall strategy. The Solutions Architecture evolves from the Business Architecture and focuses on the functional details of defined sub-sections of the Business Architecture and facilitates integration of all of the key components of the plan. This means integrating the technology, the governmental agencies involved in the implementation and the related processes concerned with procurement, financial management, and regulatory issues, etc. This architecture is critical because the Smart City involves so many different disciplines and governmental agencies. In a typical project there is a need for active involvement and integration of units involved in education, health care, land development and planning, environmental systems, commerce, airports, seaports and indeed all transportation systems,

The Business Architecture sets the stage for the next four Tasks associated with implementation and the creation of a unit that assumes responsibility for what might be called generically an "Integrated Smart City Command and Control Center."

Service Architecture

Service Architecture provides a common framework and vocabulary to characterize the technology and business components that collectively comprise a Smart City business and technology infrastructure. The Service Architecture helps the various stakeholders rapidly assemble technology solutions to solve an emerging business requirement through sharing and re-use of business and technology components. A component is a self-contained process, service or technology capability. These component parts are exposed through determining each and every key business or technology interface.

Technical Architecture

Technical Architecture provides a foundation to describe the standards, specifications and technologies supporting the delivery, exchange and construction of business or service components of each of the new business or service solutions. The Technical Architecture provides a foundation to advance the re-use of technology and components services from a citywide perspective. This process, in effect, identifies what might be called a service overlap or "underlap".

Performance Architecture

Performance Architecture is a framework to measure the performance of major Smart City initiatives and their contribution to program performance. The Performance Architecture helps to produce enhanced performance information; improve task alignment and better articulate the contribution of each key input, such as technology. The Performance Architecture also identifies desired outputs and outcomes. This process also identifies improved opportunities that span traditional city boundaries. The Discovery Card of Dundee or the integrated use of RFID tags are but two examples. Performance measurement and better articulation of those numbers is of utmost importance when trying to attract foreign investment to a new initiative.

Organizational and Management Model

People are a critical component in every initiative. It is recognized that the Organization and Management model for the Smart City cannot be planned in a vacuum. The Organizational and Management Model must include consideration of the local citizenry, governmental agencies, local business as well as global and local potential investors. While the overall aim of the Smart City often tends to be largely commercially driven, the management model must take into consideration obligations with respect to educational development and health care for the citizenry, environmental issues, concerns with energy independence, and even cultural and religious concerns.

Technology Model

The ultimately value of the Smart City is gauged not by the complexity and sophistication of its engineering, but by how people use and benefit from it. It is remarkable how the admonitions of the Greek Philosopher Alcaeus to this effect have stood the test of time ever since the 6th century B.C.

Today, the use of information technology can create a government that overcomes the barriers of time and distance to perform the business of government and provide information and services to the public. Information technology can swiftly be employed to transfer funds, answer questions, collect and validate data, and keep information flowing smoothly within and outside government. In an electronic world, high-speed information links carry the data necessary to support government operations. The development of a "SMART" infrastructure as outlined above enables the creation of "virtual agencies" which allows citizens access to integrated program information and services.

The main purpose of the Smart City model is to create a responsive infrastructure that strengthens public service delivery and enhances performance. This model allows today's public organizations to transform and integrate large quantities of data and information into a strong force of knowledge for economic growth and public service.

Infrastructure Reference Model

The various figures provided below represent a possible Infrastructure Reference Model that can be used in designing a Smart City and can be scaled to various undertakings as needed. This Model seeks to generically refer to the entities and interfaces, the service areas of the Application Platform and related services.

To support all the business and city services and applications, the Smart City Technology Infrastructure should comprise a secured broadband network for the exchange of information throughout the whole city and the coverage of all segments of the population.

Universal Infrastructure Reference Model

The universal and generic "Infrastructure Reference Model" has a number of closely interrelated parts as follows.

- **Mission Critical Applications/Services.** Mission critical applications/services implement specific end-user requirements or needs (Enhanced Services, Enhanced Communications, Electronic Commerce, Resources Management Systems, etc.). This application software may be Commercial Off The Shelf (COTS), or custom developed, or a combination of both. These are the secured systems that need to be designed to share the burden of running the cities and communities. The issue of securing these systems is addressed in greater detail in Chapter 4.

- **Mission Support Applications.** Mission Support Applications, on the other hand, provide the architectural framework for managing and disseminating information flow throughout the system and sharing information among applications.

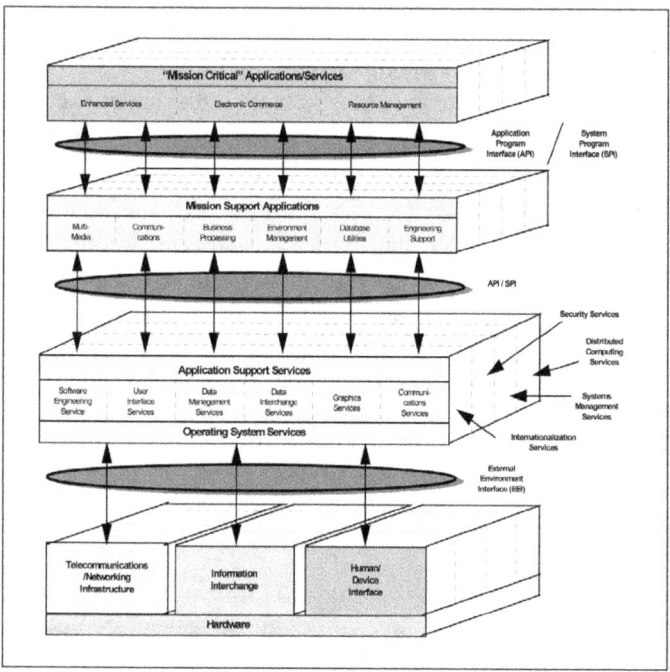

Figure 3.6: Applications and Services Required to Support a Generic Smart City

This level contains facilities for processing and displaying common data formats, and for information integration and visualization. Services in this layer tend to be mission domain specific. Support applications are common applications (e.g., E-mail, file transfer, information directories, electronic data interchange (EDI), word processing, spreadsheets) that can be standardized across individual or multiple mission areas. The services they provide can be used

- 74 -

to develop mission-area-specific applications or can be made available to the user. Support applications may be COTS products selected to provide a service in a common manner. The combination of support applications with the services of the platform layer provides the basis for a "common operating environment" to support mission applications.

- **Application Support Services.** This layer provides a characterization of the terms used to describe the Application Service Areas of the Reference Model. Described below are some of the application support services:

  - *Software Engineering Services* for system developers who require tools appropriate to the development and maintenance of applications.

  - *User Interface Services* define how users may interact with an application.

  - *Data Management Services* define how data is managed independently of the processes that create or use it, and how it can be maintained indefinitely and shared among many processes.

  - *Data Interchange Services* provide specialized support for the interchange of information between applications and to/from the external environment.

  - *Graphics Services* provide functions required for creating and manipulating pictures.

  - *Communications Services* are provided to support distributed applications requiring data access and applications interoperability in heterogeneous or homogeneous networked environments.

- *Operating System Services* are the core services needed to operate and administer the application platform and provide an interface between the application software and the platform. Application programmers will use operating system services to access operating system functions.

- **Cross Platform Services.** These services are referred to as cross platform services and have a direct effect on the operation of one or more of the application/functional service areas. In some cases, the cross platform services affect each of the functional service areas in a similar fashion, while in other cases the cross platform service has an influence that is unique to that particular service area:

  - *Internationalization Services:* As a practice, information system developers have generally designed and developed systems to satisfy a focused set of requirements that are relevant to a specific market segment. That specific market segment may be a nation or a particular cultural market. To make that information system viable, or marketable, to a different segment of the market, a full re engineering process is usually required;

  - *Security Services* are necessary to protect sensitive information in the information system. The appropriate level of protection is determined based upon the value of the information to the mission-area end users and the perception of threats to it. Information system security, for instance, is depicted as cross platform service. This is because the mechanisms implemented to provide them are typically part of multiple platform services:

- *Authentication Service* ensures system entities (e.g. processes, systems, and personnel) are uniquely identified and authenticated;

- *Access Control Service* prevents the unauthorized use of information system resources. This service also prevents the use of a resource in an unauthorized way;

- *Integrity Service* ensures protection of the system through open system integrity, network integrity, and data integrity. This ensures that data is not altered or destroyed in an unauthorized manner;

- *Confidentiality Service* ensures that data is not made available or disclosed to unauthorized individuals or computer processes through the use of data encryption, security association, and key management;

- *Non-Repudiation Services* include open systems non-repudiation, electronic signature, and electronic hashing;

- *Availability Service* ensures that timely and regular communications services are available. These services are intended to minimize delay or no delivery of data passed on communications networks.

- **System Management Services:** Information systems are composed of a wide variety of diverse resources that must be managed effectively to achieve the goals of an open system environment. While the individual resources (such as printers, software, users, processors) may differ widely, the abstraction of these resources as managed objects allows for treatment in a uniform manner.

The Internet City—The First Stage

The concept of what might be called a Smart City is, in fact, a long-term vision. Its implementation is incremental. This is not only related to costs or budgetary constraints but also because of the evolution of new technology. The first step toward implementing a Smart City might be called the creation of an "Internet City" or a city essentially based on IP architecture. This approach can provide integrated infrastructure to provide innovative applications and services in trade and commerce, tourism and education. The overall vision of a Smart City is to serve various communities of interest.

Dubai was one of the first cities to implement the integrated Internet City concept. Since then many models of Internet city have evolved. It is important to examine these models before exploring the potential of implementing an "Internet city" (i.e. one that uses universal IP architecture in provision of all electronic and information services) as a component of a Smart City.

The diagram on the next page depicts a high-level representation of the technical design for an Internet City:

The target Broadband Enterprise Infrastructure WAN/LAN Technical Model for the city integrates the existing terrestrial links and legacy network to the new architecture. Whereas there is a lack of a terrestrial infrastructure, the Core network utilizes secure broadband wireless technology to provide communication and services to all segments of business throughout the city. With a secure Gigabit bandwidth scalable core infrastructure, the Smart City will have a reliable broadband transport infrastructure to support existing and future service demands. The goal of the Smart City is to provide communication links amongst government buildings, schools, seaports, airport, businesses and enterprises, hospitals, doctors' offices and clinics, service providers, and residential areas.

The new infrastructure shall include convergence networks and systems with Enterprise Infrastructure (EI) Security (Firewall, DMZ, VPN), Data Center, Call Center, and Network Operations Center to provide services to all business platforms in the city.

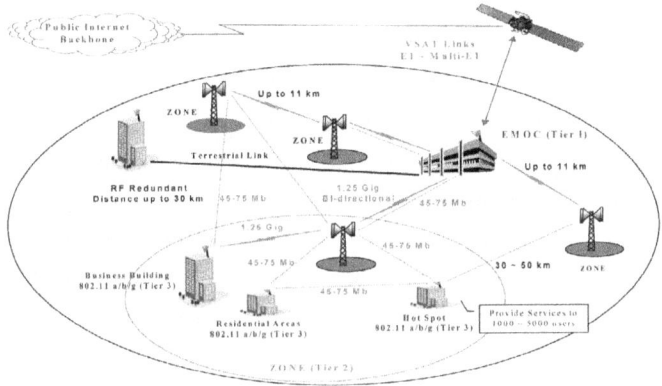

The core network would have the following generic characteristics:

- 2 Gigabit bandwidth scalable to 10 Gigabit at the Core network.

- Minimum transmitting distances between towers is 2 miles up to 4 miles with network availability of 99.9%.

The Tier 2 infrastructure would also have the following generic characteristics:

- 45 Megabit – 75 Megabit scalable bandwidth.

- Minimum transmitting distances between towers is 10 miles up to 20 miles (16 to 32 kilometers) with network availability of 99.9%.

Integrated Command and Control Center

The Smart City Integrated Command and Control Center is a solution that serves to integrate the collection, analysis, collaboration, and dissemination of all the Smart City related information to create a secure, efficient, and cost effective environment. The solution also provides an infrastructure to support value-added service providers through a Managed Service front and back office offering. These services enhance the economic environment surrounding the city, thereby helping attract and retain targeted businesses and industries, along with their associated business. The components of Smart City Command and Control Center increases the City's ability to integrate systems and operations, enhance physical security, streamline operations, and improve communications among the multiple internal and external constituencies of the larger community.

This capability naturally requires some rather sophisticated technology. The discussion below is provided for those who would like to understand the technical complexity of the information systems needed to provide universal interconnectivity and standardization of services across an entire community based on a uniform IP signaling and switching network. The specifics may vary from community to community but the model approach depicted below is a useful representation of an integrated architecture that has been proven in past projects initiated and completed by the Bearing Point Corporation. In short, those who want to stay focused on a 30,000 foot (or 10,000 meter) overview of how to plan for the future can skip to the conclusions of this chapter. For those who wish to explore the details of implementation the following section will be of particular interest.

As depicted below, one sees a summary of what has been designated the "IPC3 technology architecture". This architecture includes a Port with a Command and Control (CC) Engine, a Predictive Analysis and Intelligent Rules

(PAIR) Engine, a Business Intelligence (BI) Engine, and an integration fabric that links the CC, PAIR and BI engines to port security, port operations and external entities.

IPC³ Technology Architecture

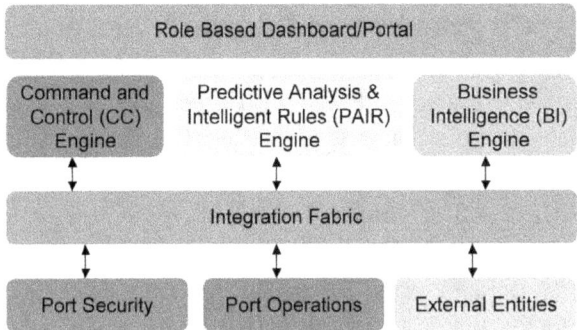

The CC Engine continually gathers data from port security, port operations and external entities to provide near real-time information about the Port. The CC Module includes a portal and an enterprise information processor. The portal provides a personalized, role-based user interface, enabling users to customize the portal to meet their management needs. The enterprise information processor constantly transforms the collected data into useful information, which enables Port operators to efficiently monitor the port.

Sense and Respond Center

The Smart City Sense & Respond Center (SCSRC) is the core component of the Smart City solution. The SCSRC will not only meet the requirement for a technical infrastructure that supports a safe, reliable, cost effective innovation area, but also helps transform the Smart City surrounding area into a highly competitive regional distribution hub and the surrounding area into a safe and secured environment. SCSRC provides new flexibility to city management to maintain the safety of it citizens and its business. The integrated command and control features of SCSRC allow management to be aware of any problem or concern and immediately take action and mediate the risk. The sense and respond component of SCSRC can also help to route resources to prevent incidents before they can occur, or mitigate the results of incidents in a timely manner.

Smart City Sense and Respond Center

A Smart City Sense and Respond Center has a least 5 core objectives: Prepare, Prevent, Detect, Protect/Defend, Mitigate/Respond, and Collaborate. They are executed through seven functions:

- Overall Security
- Awareness
- Critical Infrastructure Protection
- Dignitary Protection
- Emergency Preparedness and Response
- Counter Terrorism
- Transportation Security

An interdisciplinary consolidated Smart City Sense and Respond Center is designed to facilitate the total functionality of call taking and responding to events as they are taking place. The SCRC also obtains events information from automated sensors that is installed at various strategic locations. Depending on the business case and the triggering event these automated sensors can trigger an alarm or send an email to the respective authority to show up on the SCRC display screens. This allows for sharing information across responder agencies, quick access to the triggering event, better coordination between the responders, quick and decisive response and a more efficient use of SCRC personnel and equipment.

Enterprise architects typically will exploit two broad types of events, each having multiple subtypes. The broad typing process differentiates between strategic events and tactical events. Strategic events need quick and decisive response. Tactical events are typically used as a way of tracking and later performing business and security intelligence.

Smart City Implementation

Smart City applications and services can help enhance the security of a city, protect citizens and businesses, improve health and education services, facilitate government services, and link the community to the national and global economy. The Smart City concept is rapidly becoming a competitive tool for local and regional growth, leading to new and enhanced economic and social opportunities for citizens and businesses alike.

Implementation requires a step-by-step approach including the following:

- Develop a vision and strategy closely aligned with the both the citizenry and business and economic objectives.

- Develop blueprints for modern communication and information infrastructure and architecture to support the city applications and services.

- Determine appropriate applications and services to cater to the city's current and future business needs and to support city's socio-economic development directions.

- Develop the architecture, design, and plans for an "Intelligent Port," including enhanced Sea-Port and Airport security and safe commerce platforms utilizing tools such as the IPC3 Technology Architecture and modern communication and information technologies as provided as a useful example of a specific implementation strategy.

- Integrate existing and evolving city technology infrastructure and applications into an integrated platform to increase efficiency and cost-effectiveness.

- Develop alliances with key partners/investors and seek widespread participation.

- Full-scale implementation.

Implementation must be carefully planned and managed. The following guidelines are based on years of experience in implementing Smart City projects around the world:

- Establish a long-term vision.

- Develop a Strategic Roadmap.

- Develop a strategic plan for phased migration toward a Smart City.

- Establish a market-driven direction and seek to achieve a proper balance between public and private interests.

- Establish a single, cohesive structure to coordinate the overall implementation.

- Implement advanced, common and competitive communication and information infrastructure in partnership with the private sector.

- Initiate integrated applications and pilot projects at the earliest possible time

- Create widespread public awareness, education and training.

Conclusion

There is always a challenge for organizations facing large-scale and longer-term implementation plans that bridge their current state to an expected future state. Implementation of the systems required to achieve a Smart City is no exception. Often, the number or difficulty of tasks seems too large to overcome. The challenge lies in determining an actionable plan broken down into reasonable component parts. For each of these major component parts it is necessary to assess the benefits, costs, and risks that are involved. After this is done it is important to develop a risk mitigation plan. Finally, it is key to prioritize these initiatives based on an "impact versus effort" analysis. Ultimately one develops a complete plan, including risk mitigation that shows the specific initiatives (i.e. the major component parts) to be undertaken.

The complete plan indicates the purpose of each of the initiatives and their priority sequencing and interdependencies. It shows the scope of work to be done, the area of responsibility, and the estimated cost for complete implementation. The resulting set of initiatives can be classified into Foundational, Adoptive, and Transformational components. This classification further assists the organization in both understanding their current state and realizing the amount of effort that needs to be undertaken to move the organization all the way to a complete transformation into a Smart City over a period of a number of years. If done in proper sequence the benefits will unfold in a constructive manner that makes the city more efficient and productive over time. This will allow the process to gain increasing momentum and success will breed further success.

Selected Bibliography

Bell, Robert. "The Top Seven Intelligent Communities of 2008." Intelligent Community Forum: 14 January 2008.

Jung, John G. "Towards Creating an Intelligent Taiwan – The Global ICF Experience." International Digital Cities Conference: Taoyuan, Taiwan, August 11-14, 2008.

Komninos, Nicos. "Strategy: Singapore-Intelligent Nation 2015." 26 August 2008.

www.urenio.org/2008/08/26/strategy-singapore-intelligent-nation-2015

Mitchell, William M. "Smart City 2020." *BusinessWeek*: 11 April 2006.

Mitchell, William M. "Intelligent Cities". Inaugural Lecture of the UOC 2007-08 Academic Year: No. 5, Oct. 2007.

www.uoc.edu/uocpapers/5/dt/eng/mitchell.pdf

Tsarchopoulos, Panagiotis. "Building the Zero-Emission City." 13 May 2008.

www.urenio.org/2008/05/13/building-the-zero-emissions-city

Tsarchopoulos, Panagiotis. "Gangnam District in Seoul Named the Intelligent Community of the Year.": 21 May 2008.

www.urenio.org/2008/05/21/gangnam-district-in-seoul-named-the-intelligent-community-of-the-year/#more-775

CHAPTER 4

Safety and Security in the Future City

By Christine Robinson

Chapter in Brief

The advent of terrorist attacks around the world seems to have only escalated since the catastrophic attacks of September 11, 2001. Most articles and books written about urban security in recent years have thus rather predictably focused on means to avoid such types of terrorist threats. This chapter, however, seeks to address more broadly how modern cities with complex technical systems can be conceived and implemented so as to achieve a number of goals and objectives related to providing greater security to their citizenry. This means trying to design the cities of the future so that they are less vulnerable to natural disasters or terrorist attacks. It also means a "paradigm shift" in our thinking in terms of how we conceive of, plan for and implement strategies to achieve what might be called the "future city." Finally, at a philosophical level, it tries to address the very meaning of "security" for all people living and working in the city of the future.

Christine Robinson, award-winning author and industry leader, is internationally recognized for her contributions to Enterprise Architecture, Business Process Management and Emergency Preparedness-Disaster Recovery. Christine consults independently to industry and government, and previously worked for CSC as a principal consultant, as well as for Verizon, SAIC and Nextel. On a volunteer basis, she serves as an appointed commission member on the Arlington County Information Technology Advisory Commission.

Charles Darwin said that it would be neither the strongest nor the most intelligent that would survive, but those most adaptable to change. Effective change and flexibility are at the very heart of the planning for the safety and security of the "future city." Systematic planning for a better city is an intricate, complex and holistic enterprise as well as an ongoing challenge. One must start by recognizing that this task is more than just deploying sophisticated technology. The first key is providing power to the people (i.e. the users) rather than power to complex technological systems. The second key is to integrate overall system planning and technology upgrades with security and safety objectives. This is opposed to the conventional way of seeing management and efficiency upgrading activities as separate and perhaps competing objectives vis a vis safety and security. Figure 4.1 below illustrates the difference in attitude and management philosophy that are implicit in the two schools of thought.

Figure 4.1
"Power to the People" Versus "Power to Complex Technological Systems"

"Power to the People"	Key Decision Elements	"Power to the Machines"
Decentralized and Accessible Systems	System Architecture	Highly Centralized
Individual Physiological Characteristics	Access to Secure Systems	Highly Complex Codes with Frequent Updates
Telework Options	Work Location	Required Office Attendance for All Jobs
Flex Time	Work Schedule	Rigid Work Week
PDAs, palmtop computers, 4 G cellphones	IT and Communications Facilities	Desktop computers or mainframes and wireline telephones
Letting Employees Leverage Electronic and IT Security	Safety and Security	Putting Employees and Files in a Physically Protected Space

The new approach requires integrated and flexible planning that involves all elements of the community—that is to say citizens, business, and government. This approach involves the ability to adapt and update the overall plan as the actual benefits—and strengths and weaknesses—of the vision are revealed. Creating a community that is better, smarter, and "greener", as well as safer and more secure involves a holistic approach that views objectives as mutually reinforcing rather than competing strategies.

If this new approach is taken we will indeed see a paradigm shift where cities proceed to modernize, upgrade and modernize management techniques and use information technology tools more effectively. At the same time they can also devise urban communities that are safer and more secure. To be successful, these upgrades and management shifts must work at many different levels. They must subsume in the process many different organizations and succeed in effectively inter-twining them. Out of the piece-parts of many different organizations, a holistic picture must emerge without killing creativity, individual initiative, or widely varying goals and missions.

A Critical Paradigm Shift

We are in the midst of a paradigm shift where parties on many levels have begun to realize that it is possible to build security and emergency preparedness and disaster recovery capabilities into everyday activities. Indeed this approach is beginning to become more and more prevalent. The basic concepts are now set forth under a formal U.S. Homeland Security initiative. The same approach could and should hold true for cities, regions, states, and other formal and informal urban planning umbrellas and mechanisms. This approach, that is now gaining ever-widening acceptance, looks at a city holistically. It examines how one can use integrated technology tools while still maintaining initiative, individuality and even maintaining geographic decentralization.

One can use such creative IT tools to upgrade operations, improve energy efficiency and productivity, make transportation systems more effective, leverage education and health care capabilities without a loss of creativity on a macro and micro level. At the same time, the work and community environment can benefit from increased safety and security as well. If this is done well, with a process which includes the input of the community, citizens, workers, business people and governmental representatives, the results can be relatively rapid and with measurable benefits. In short, an approach that is holistic, with significant input from all the players, as well as flexible and up-datable should be able to produce a city that is more efficient smarter, greener, and more secure. It should have educational, training and health care systems that produce better results at lower costs. All of these results create a populace that is more prosperous, better informed, and in lots of subtle ways better protected against natural disaster, crime or even terrorist attack.

Instead of the typical distributed group of experts operating in separate stove-pipes, we can enable architects, urban planners, electrical and computer engineers, educators, health care workers, transportation and energy workers, and more, to jointly evolve a coordinated holistic approach to making cities better—in ways that include safer and more secure.

Recommended steps in this regard are:

- Planners and managers who are seeking to achieve the so-called "paradigm shift" must develop a high level picture by getting extensive input from throughout the city. They must not only develop a comprehensive overview but also drill down to finite details of city and other operations,

- Experts and various stakeholders on more of a micro level must have their own sets of rules and processes to manage and study their environments that all comprise piece-parts of a holistic enterprise. At the same time, they must be able to achieve economies of scale in terms of using efficient broadband systems, allow telework options to service employees and adopt security systems that are effective but not burdensome.

- Planners should look at a city with all of its components on a macro and micro level and within the larger context of global, national, provincial, and local factors (including trade, trade deficits, commodity exports and imports, intellectual property and its protection, sources of financing, and strategic considerations). All of these characteristics and influences should be built into the planning processes,

- The resulting strategic business and security plan must be inclusive of all aspects of government, business, community residents and workers, non-profit organizations, citizenry, and those who may work or do business in the city who may not be citizens but contribute to the economy.

This "holistic" methodology would allow planners to study the police and fire departments, other first responders, the school and health care systems, the various other elements of city government, the current and projected businesses and tax base, etc. The task is to consider them as inter-related parts. These inter-related parts join together through business rules, business practices, financing systems, and public laws and practices that make up the systems that will ultimately run the future city and enable it to become safer and more secure.

Benefits To Taking
An Enterprise Approach

By looking at the city as an enterprise powered by technology tools as opposed to separate and distinct pieces, the planners and stakeholders of the future city can exponentially improve the means by which the city can make itself more efficient, more energy independent, and more responsive to its citizenry and business (in terms of online hours of operation and accessibility, for instance) but also safer and more secure. The city can respond more effectively to various security and safety incidents by devising realistic scenarios from data collected from first responders at the scene of an attack or crime or through various "smart sensor data" gathered automatically. This information can be shared with first responders and public officials via the Internet and variously devised web sites.

Each facet of city operations become an input into the ongoing planning process as business rules, business practices, trade statistics, energy consumption, traffic congestion and overloads on the education and health care systems are identified and responded to by urban officials. In essence, one of the keys to effective "enterprise management" is for planners and other participants to have better access to timely data through linking to other systems such as logistics systems, supply-chain systems and other data sources on a need-to-know basis which would assure access would be available only to approved parties.

Planners and managers alike can more quickly capture and analyze the effects of current and evolving policies and other influences on a city's society and infrastructure by identifying them as rules within the technology management system which would then govern which processes to automatically set in motion according to which rule is applied. Planners using the technology management tools can obtain more up-to-date reporting on cause and effect than typical manual processes offer. By gathering information and using this for study purposes, this can help predict outcomes of future policies and process improvements with far greater speed and effectiveness. Technology tools will enable planners and stakeholders alike to have ready access to resulting data and outcomes of policies, studies, etc. versus having to wait extended periods of time, as we do now, to obtain information and results of a particular field of study.

We can ensure greater fairness in addressing the needs of often over-looked members of the society such as the handicapped, children, elderly, language challenged and others by including their needs and pre-plan responses with specially crafted response capabilities.

The future city can thus become less of a victim to the vagaries of the political system and rely more upon inputs as guidelines, laws, etc. residing in software that can swiftly change the nature and magnitude of emergency response depending on what rules are in force. This enterprise approach uses technology management tools built on the basis of actual experience from communities that have experienced a particular natural disaster, attack or various man-made crises or environmental endangerment. This approach serves to place the power and the response modes more in the hands of the people: (i) who are responsible for doing the day to day work, (ii) those who contributed to designing the emergency response processes, and (iii) those officially in charge of the various public safety and security agencies.

The planning processes can ultimately become much more understandable and visible to everyone so that government and citizens alike can better understand what each other needs in order to perform their respective responsibilities before, during, and after an emergency. The training processes can also be much more closely targeted to actually recorded circumstances. This is critical since emergencies are a "come as you are party". This means if people are not trained as to recovery processes or in the use of particular communications or rescue equipment, recovery will be slower or less effective than desired. This process can be as mundane as getting proper credentials not only to fire and police personnel but also to power, gas, or communications repair personnel, training first responders on satellite phones, or testing public safety announcement and alert systems. Rescuers will be better able to provide critical information and resources they and other parties require that would enable everyone to protect themselves better and help make the environment safer for others.

All training within the "Enterprise Approach" involves more than just first responders. The public needs to be "trained" to sign up for "first alert" systems, to be encouraged to have emergency response kits and supplies, and to know where to tune battery operated radios for emergency instructions.

Instead of acting in a "serial fashion" as emergency operations often occur in today's world, this new approach will enable far more activities to occur in parallel, because work groups can pre-plan many activities that are automatically enacted through technology management tools and can enable planners to generate responses for unforeseen circumstances in real-time. The ability for emergency command centers to change two-way corridors into one-way roadways for evacuations, to immediately call up pandemic treatment centers, to dial up real time information on noxious gas sensors or check immediately on meteorological conditions in a specific neighborhood are capabilities that have to be planned. Training for rapid and parallel responses to crises is essential.

For instance, police, fire and other first responders can input data into a system that indicates what type of response is required, notifies the responders and others of the situation and findings, assigns the transportation and other resources, and can provide situational awareness concerning an event. Such a capability can enable responses to occur for more quickly and automatically delegate as much of the routine tasks and decision-making to the technology tools. Capabilities that allow a command center to know instantly what police, fire or other first responders are located where and to be able to communicate with them in real time is just one of the capabilities that a future city should have. Back-up command centers, emergency power generators, emergency communications devices not dependent on conventional power supplies, and other capabilities are listed in federal emergency response guidelines.

Enterprise Management, Decentralization, and Telecommuting

The urban planners for the future city will encourage workers and employers to decentralize. This means providing incentives and support for practices such as telecommuting. This practice, for instance, needs to be seen in a "holistic" sense. Such practices help to avoid congestion, reduce accidents, reduce carbon emissions, and help to eliminate highly centralized targets such as the Pentagon or the London Stock Exchange building as a target for terrorists.

Enterprise management allows decentralization into communities where people work and live yet without excessively long commutes and harm to the environment.

Smart broadband systems allow greater efficiency, better use of time, and even promote autonomy among communities of interest right down to specific details of particular agencies or businesses while still benefiting from IT based economies of scale. Such practices can make communities less like likely to become targets and would allow a less concentrated number of people to occupy a given area, making urban civilizations more impervious to attack.

Emergency Preparedness and Response

Interoperable communications are another key component of an "enterprise managed" system. This is a design capability critical to helping cities become safer and more secure. This approach provides the ability to communicate by computer, plain old telephone service (POTS) lines, cell phones, Blackberries, and radios of various protocols and across multiple bands. With this level of interoperability it becomes vastly simpler to communicate between various responder groups who may all have their own individual technologies that don't talk to one another.

A lack of clarity as to who is in charge in today's world can also complicate emergency response. Participants and first responders can waste precious time trying to identify the appropriate authorities in charge for specific circumstances. Not having interoperable communications between different groups often exacerbates the problem of determining who is in charge and deciding on appropriate action to take. An enterprise management system helps to interpret the data provided to it and sets forth optimum courses of action. For instance, the rules would dictate that fire department and police would respond to a house fire, whereas if evidence pointed toward a terrorist attack, the system would automatically identify and alert the appropriate response team. Such an interoperable communications system plus instant access to a rich database indicating appropriate responses to a variety of attacks from bio-terrorism, kidnapping, or an explosion can be very helpful, particularly in areas where multiple authorities might have jurisdiction.

A clear process for determination of who is in charge and rapid setting in motion of pre-defined response plans can serve to improve emergency preparedness and response. Access to these tools, plus the ability to communicate regardless of electronic means available to first responders, undoubtedly serves to improve the ability of responders and incident commanders to take action according to who is in charge and to perform their duties accordingly. Such a universal and interoperable communications capability allows all responders to be able to coordinate their activities, according to their respective role. A well-designed enterprise management system can provide clear authority for access, across sometimes disparate communications media and help coordinate their activities in a more seamless fashion. This can drastically reduce the duplication of effort on the part of multiple parties who might respond to an event, avoid confusion, eliminate wasted time and resources, and increase overall efficiency to those responding to security or safety crises. It can also call up resources from adjacent communities and federal authorities. This could be additional human resources and first responders or it could prioritize the call for additional specialized equipment such as mobile units to identify people under collapsed buildings in the case of an earthquake or an explosion.

As noted earlier, one of the key aspects of emergency preparedness and response is training people prior to a disruption so that they know ahead of time what they are supposed to do during an emergency and how to access and operate specialized equipment. Training them in how, when, and with whom they should respond is absolutely critical to success in real live situations.

Just in the Washington Metropolitan Area, authorities need to manage communications from such groups as multiple police and fire departments across jurisdictions as well as Federal authorities from a broad cross-section of agencies with varying responsibilities, depending on the type and severity of an event. This may require interoperable communications and disaster response coordination involving the Department of Defense, Homeland Security personnel, including the Coast Guard and the Federal Emergency Management Administration (FEMA) plus many other first responder organizations from the Red Cross or Red Crescent, to aid-providing non-governmental organizations, and even to various satellite communications organizations. Large port cities around the world and in the U.S. also have a significant problem with having to deal with multiple governing authorities who may think they are in charge and need to communicate between their various organizations. Interoperable communications coupled with an appropriate technology management capability will be highly useful. Such capabilities combined with training allows the best hope for an effective response to an emergency or other situation where pre-defined response scenarios and coordinated responses can save time and increase the effectiveness of the rescue operation in real time.

Many communities of interest need to provide input into the planning and testing of emergency response solutions. Those involved in developing the pre-defined responses and identifying all the resources needed to carry them out is a large and diverse group. The critical planners include the medical community, transportation officials, school officials, communications, utilities and other business people, and a myriad of other potential contributors.

These individuals and organizations need to be involved to determine the detailed information on types of personnel required for response, types of transportation required, medical supplies, food, and much more as part of the emergency preparedness and response community.

Technology Tools

The cities that adopt an enterprise approach can thus be much better prepared. They can build in self-healing mechanisms through planning and implementing IT and communications systems as well as by designing technology management tools that use appropriate response rules, specific recovery policies, and establish defined thresholds. Some refer to these thresholds in certain types of disciplines such as IT as Service Level Agreements (SLA) and each functional area could have its own SLA. The police, fire department, health care and EMT first responders, and other types of organizations can all have pre-defined SLAs that identify the time within which they must appear on the scene, the types of services they can provide, the time allowed before calling in other backups and resources, and much more. These SLAs can become a part of how the city automatically responds to emergencies and executes pre-defined response scenarios.

One of the most important points we all need to understand about technology is that it is not the technology itself that solves the crises. No, the key is in critical thinking about who, where and when to use the technology and how to deploy it so it is accessible. Just as important is training people as to how they can best harness these technologies. Just having the technologies alone is no guarantee that they will be of any use. Leaders and technicians alike need to understand that just using technology without having the right skills to make the most of it will just cause more frustration, more mis-steps, and less than optimal use of scarce resources. In the case of the Katrina Hurricane disaster, there were instances of first responders hauling around satellite telephones in their cars but never using them because they had never been trained in their use.

The public telecommunications infrastructure and the emergency communications networks will increasingly be based on Internet protocol (IP) systems. These IP networks will support an increasing percentage of all utilities. Networks for governments, businesses, the citizenry and first responders around the world will be essentially all IP based because of the cost effectiveness, efficiencies, and global interconnectivity involved.

The combination of broadband technologies with faster and more efficient connections plus Internet Protocol switching that can transmit data over electronic networks from and to just about any system imaginable gives us unprecedented communications. The phrase "anytime and anywhere communications" has now become a reality on most of our planet.

These communications systems linked together with the best and most responsive technology management tools can largely become the brains of the "future city." These systems will need human oversight and will need to be designed by all of the communities of interests outlined above. These systems, once well designed and tested, can become a key element in the safety and security of the future city. Within the IT world now and in the future, applications software packages that run, in isolation, various disjointed aspects of a city's operations will become less important as these technology management tools become more powerful and integrated and begin to take the place of different types of applications software more and more. The danger here in developing these powerful and integrated tools, is that the planning and control process becomes overly centralized. One of the keys to the longer-term effectiveness of these IT tools will be in achieving cost efficiency and economies of scale, but at the same time allowing distributed architectures that allow optimization for various human goals and specific services unique to a particular neighborhood, company, or artistic endeavor.

The most successful Future Cities will make more extensive and wise use of technology tools to promote diversity of applications and human services. These tools will be used to improve the effectiveness of government, business, planners, and citizens alike. It will require a delicate balance to trade off efficiency and interoperability with neighborhood identity and distributed services responsive to individual communities and artistic and cultural diversity.

Future Cities can literally run their normal operations by incorporating critical information from utilities, city services, transportation infrastructure, the private sector, government, and other inter-related organizations that will impact the security of the community. Planners can plan small operations using technology tools and leadership can run the city in normal operations as well as emergency operations from a macro level. This approach will help reduce chaos and confusion often surrounding emergency responses and use resources more wisely.

Information security software currently represents one of the fastest growing segments of the software industry and will have an increasing importance in protecting the security of the future city. Information security software can not only protect the information systems the city government run, but just as important, it can enable other segments such as the utilities to better protect themselves, such as from the hacking incident that knocked out the power grid in the Northeastern region of the United States in 2003.

Just having the information security software does not mean a city is protected. We must have highly skilled and trained human resources available to run the information security programs and establish appropriate thresholds for different types of responses. They must also understand how and when to blow the whistle if there should be an abuse of power or to sound an alert if a vulnerability in the network is detected or there is an inappropriate response to an attack.

Information sharing between various entities will become even more prevalent and is highly key to our safety and security. Establishing secure access to information resources will help reduce redundancy and duplication and allow people to work more efficiently by sharing information.

Let us take the example of the law enforcement community. In order to be effective, various agencies at the local, state, national and international level must coordinate with multiple parties and would ideally share information across jurisdictions. Just within the law enforcement community in the U.S., authorities need access to data from Federal databases, local crime reports, federal records, and DNA reports, just to name a few.

Having each organization keep its own separate sources of information or limit access to information for those who need it will impede progress toward keeping cities safe. This limits the ability to identify and apprehend those parties whose crimes or information may be known to other entities but who may not be aware of other offenses. Law enforcement officials will be better able to catch criminals and manage law enforcement cases through dramatically improved access to shared data among different jurisdictions on a local, state, national, and international basis.

At the same time safeguards need to developed and maintained. There must be a process of auditing records and correcting them. In Sweden, public databases are capable of being destroyed on a moment's notice if necessary. This is in memory of the history where public records were used by Nazi investigators to track down and persecute those of the Jewish religion. Again efficiency must be balanced against protection of rights. Instant response must be balanced against sensitive records being used in an illegal or abusive way against the very citizenry that these records were meant to protect.

Law enforcement operations must be optimized to ensure a protection of individual rights and accuracy on one hand and rapid and effective response to emergency conditions on the other. These activities must involve the development of rules and processes that balance, preserve and protect efficiency goals against individual liberties. One must hope that the future city information processes will give greater weight to liberty and freedom than it will to speed and efficiency of operations.

Certainly some efficiency gains in emergency responses have clear value to everyone and should not abridge individual rights in any significant way. Police and fire can intelligently pre-define their response plans and develop careful emergency scenarios to disasters that can be foresee. These plans, coordinated with the citizenry and caregivers will be initiated when triggered by pre-established thresholds.

First responders will know in advance and be trained to perform certain tasks. Law enforcement officials, fire fighters, EMT technicians, and so on will be able to coordinate and act more efficiently as the technology management tools present appropriate responses. Law enforcement officials will be far better able to coordinate efforts between various departments and jurisdictions because they will have access to process-driven models governed by business rules that have been developed with care and adapted to experience and citizen and business concerns over time.

In today's world, too often organizations risk the privacy of data for individuals and other entities because they don't understand the implications and don't use good security practices. Successful future cities will obtain the skilled and highly trained resources who understand how to make a city safe and secure; and to apply biometrics, secure access, sensors, forensics, and other specialized areas to secure the city.

Utilities also represent a very important component of a city as they provide the energy needed by homes, businesses, and government and their absence can create chaos for every element of a city. A lapse can even cause death in the case of people on life support, accidents because traffic signals don't work, and the inconvenience of not being able to turn on the air conditioning or the heat during a power blackout.

Protecting the safety and security of utilities is also key because without energy, water, and gas, life changes dramatically. The energy community has at times been criticized for its lack of sophistication and understanding of how to provide the information security to protect its systems from being hacked into. The future city leaders will encourage the utilities to improve their skills to better defend their systems.

There needs to be a systematic attempt to provide the security of the many utilities on which we depend. Again this protection for dams, power companies, nuclear power plants, gas companies, water providers, and more must consider more than physical protection.

All of these utility systems are ultimately controlled by IT systems. This infrastructure will remain inherently vulnerable unless they are more thoroughly protected than they are today.

Future cities can incorporate data coming from utilities into technology management tools that run their normal operations as well as their emergency planning and response. Just as in other segments, planners and utilities can create pre-planned scenarios to handle power outages, gasoline explosions, nuclear emissions, and other calamities so that when they receive data about emergencies they automatically activate the emergency plans and respond as quickly and efficiently as possible.

Sensor Management and Regional and National Alerts

Cities such as Washington, DC, New York, Boston, San Francisco, San Diego, London, Tokyo, and other major cities around the world are comprised of a multitude of boroughs, counties, cities, and many other formal organizations such as port authorities, water districts, school districts, fire districts, to name just a few, and present exorbitantly complex management issues. Imagine the difficulty officials just in New York City have in managing complex operations within and between all the different entities in the five boroughs within New York City, not to mention, New Jersey. Boat traffic entering the harbor, air traffic landing in New York City and New Jersey, and ground transportation all represent potential threats to the homes and work places of everyone located in or near them. They also can provide endless sources of sensor data identifying what goods and products these various vehicles may be carrying. Bridges and tunnels are alive 24 hours a day carrying vast numbers of people and transporting cargo.

Biological, chemical, radiological, infrared, and nuclear sensors plus a myriad other "intelligent" devices and detectors now supply billions of bits of data for guardians of the public safety to monitor and transmit. These separate systems often don't share data with others who might need to know about potential threats and respond to them. It is a particular challenge to better understand how to share this data and carefully manage who can access the data, especially to make sure that it reaches those who need it while protecting individual rights against warrantless eavesdropping and surveillance.

It is difficult to imagine the complexity involved in trying to gather this diverse information, let alone to manage all the possible data inputs that each of these areas of possible threats provide every day and night. Managing sensor data at an "optimum level" and then to provide it immediately to those who need it and who have a need-to-know is a true challenge. At the technology level there is a difficult question of human versus "machine assessment" of threat conditions. In light of the huge amount of data involved some level of analysis and assessment will undoubtedly be carried out through the use of artificial intelligence and "smart computer programs" as well as which business rules govern a particular condition. An even greater challenge is deciding how much assessment is necessary and appropriate in a democratic society. At some point there can be a real possibility of information overload and missing a major threat by trying to collect too much data. There is a famous statement that says that if one monitors the security of diamonds and paper clips with equal vigor that the likely result is that we will lose a great many more diamonds.

Each organization or jurisdiction might have particular rules of engagement and processes for responding to what might be a nuclear, biological, natural disaster, or some other type of threat. Organizations can pre-define their responses that will automatically execute with as little human intervention as possible upon identifying a potential major threat. This helps take out much of the guesswork. The technology management tools can coordinate and manage a regional response as well as an individual organization's response, but care must be taken to devise such plans with significant local input. Further, if a potential threat becomes a "real threat" then human responders must be on alert to carry out remediation plans as quickly as possible.

For example, major metropolitan areas could share sensor data from different sources to better determine where and how a potential threat may present itself and then provide a coordinated and appropriate response. Each type of response might require a different type of personnel resources and different types of equipment. For each type of emergency it is prudent to identify a specific set of tasks and responses as well as a listing of needed equipment and the qualifications of response teams. A biological alarm might require some of the same or many other different sets of pre-defined processes and associated resources compared to a radiological, nuclear, weather, or other type of threat. In the United States, in the wake of not only 9/11 but other natural disasters, a National Incident Response Framework has been activated. This includes the use of capabilities of the Department of Homeland Security, the Department of Defense and the Federal Bureau of Investigation, as well as the Environmental Protection Agency (EPA), the U.S. Department of Energy, the Nuclear Regulatory Commission, the Department of Agriculture (USDA) and the Center for Disease Control (CDC). Responses for any or all of these agencies can be "triggered" by specific sensor data alerts and pre-planned responses can be mapped out for various types of emergencies. Likewise State and local agencies can also be activated in the specific geographic areas that are affected. Efforts are now underway for an increasing number of these "intelligent emergency alert sensors" to be interconnected by the Internet and thus linked to targeted web sites and emergency call centers.

This type of Internet-based system that integrates information between disaster alert sensor systems and disseminates data to pre-targeted agencies is currently in use by the US Military. In many cases emergency coordinators, 911 center operators, and others who have a role in providing community safety and security can create their own alert systems simply by obtaining the necessary Commercial-Off-the Shelf (or COTS) products. They then need to integrate their emergency alert systems with the national systems and use them under recommended guidelines. Cities can avail themselves of these same types of technologies in this fashion and link into U.S. Military and other parts of the U.S. Government simply by using a secure broadband Internet connection with assigned security access privileges. In order for cities to successfully exploit such systems they do need to harness the skilled personnel who understand these capabilities and use potential incident alerts in a professional and responsible manner.

This type of technology management system can automatically execute pre-defined processes and identify and alert those resources needed to respond to a particular type of alert upon receipt of sensor data. This approach will exponentially improve cities' and regions' ability to detect threats via sensors from a multitude of sources within and across jurisdictional boundaries, share data to best advantage, and act far more efficiently. For instance, data about potential radiological threats could automatically feed into sensors linked by an Internet-based system that assimilates data from all different types of sensors supplied by multiple jurisdictions and authorities. This could quickly help to identify the geographic range of a particular emergency.

The technology management tools would determine on a pre-defined basis whether or not a response is required and what it might be. It could also help identify those organizations that should respond to the threat, how they would respond, and where. The Environmental Protection Agency (EPA), the Nuclear Regulatory Commission, local police, FBI, health officials, and many more might each have defined roles to play in responding to data collected from radiological sensors. Cities can prepare likely scenarios to fit their own unique needs.

Sensor management could become in many ways akin to the process of gathering and processing other types of data. In such a case managers would likely input the rules and pre-define the responses appropriate for each type of threat identified via sensors. Emergency response teams would also likely be put on urgent alert.

Serving Special Needs Populations

It is possible to improve planning and response for Special Needs Populations to minimize or avoid the highly publicized situations that occurred during and after Hurricane Katrina. In this disaster, handicapped and disabled people were abandoned by their caretakers and left to fend for themselves or in some cases even die. It is now possible to plan to meet the needs of this particular population and far better equip emergency personnel than ever before.

Certainly a paradigm shift is needed to meet effectively the needs of an extremely varied Special-Needs-Population in emergency conditions.

This includes individuals with disabilities, special medical and dietary needs, the elderly, children, people from diverse cultural backgrounds, the transportation disadvantaged, and non English speaking people or those who are limited in speaking English well enough to communicate and comprehend instructions.

The Robert T. Stafford Disaster Relief and Emergency Assistance Act enacted in the United States in 1988 states that special needs populations cannot be denied or deprived from any FEMA program whether it is direct assistance or through any state or local government, and educational institutions. Any other board or institution receiving federal emergency funding would have the same requirement not to deny assistance.

Clearly the intent of this law was not met in several recent disasters in the U.S. As a consequence of Hurricane Katrina, in particular, federal agencies have been charged with strengthening planning for needs of people with disabilities. FEMA established the role of Disability Coordinator following the enactment of the 2006 Post Katrina Emergency Management Reform Act.

In response to this act it has been determined that the special needs population in an emergency response situation may need such support mechanisms as:

- Medication and facilities for mentally ill patients,

- Medication, facilities, and supplies for patients under medical care,

- Medical equipment such as kidney dialysis machines, IV, heart monitors, wheel chairs, to name a few,

- Knowledge about the schedules and special needs for each individual,

- Matching the appropriate personnel and skills required to care for these special needs individuals,

- Interpreters who can communicate with those who are not fluent in English or other local languages if in other countries,

- Sign language interpreters for the deaf,

- Child care professionals, and

- Transportation for people who do not have cars or other means of transportation to carry them out of harm's way.

The enterprise approach enabled through technology tools holds powerful implications for the handicapped and disabled whose needs can be even more complicated than the general populace. This population is generally less able to fend for themselves in an emergency. The ability to create pre-planned scenarios specifically for the handicapped and disabled as well as create new plans in real time can greatly enable responders to help this segment of the population. Clearly such planning and capabilities must be an essential part of planning for a truly effective future city.

For instance, planning for emergency situations must provide for instantaneous access to information about logistics, the Internet, various supply-chains, transportation, medical resources, and readily accessible communications and power capabilities. In short, a "smart" or "future" city must plan and implement capabilities for normal times, but also must plan and make provision for an effective emergency response tailored to people with special needs as well as for the mainstream population.

One of the Post-Katrina adjustments that has been made to emergency response procedures in the U.S. has been to officially require a capability to respond not only to the needs of people but also to make arrangements for the safety of animals and pets, since many people refuse to abandon them even in a time of great crisis. It became widely known that many people stayed behind during Hurricane Katrina because they would have had to leave their pets behind. The Special Needs Populations can't take care of themselves as readily as mainstream populations and may not normally contribute to typical planning processes due to the nature of their circumstances and conditions. Therefore, garnering the support and enlisting the aid of those who care for and interact with the Special-Needs-Populations is crucial to successful planning. In short, establishing effective plans for Special Needs Populations may require more interaction and intervention on the part of the larger community to assure successful plans. A number of organizations using paid and unpaid resources within the faith-based and community groups, social service organizations, neighborhood associations and others have strong relationships and have established a basis of trust among those they support. These organizations are thus critical to include in the planning process, but often may be a part of the support infrastructure during a time of emergency.

Certain trends indicate that Special Needs Populations will continue to grow in countries of the OECD. More people are increasingly moving to areas that are higher risk due to coastal storms with more and more people of increasing age living in coastal counties. The population of OECD countries is aging and with increased age comes increasing incidences of Special-Needs-Populations who are not as able to fend for themselves. On a global basis the percentage of cities that have a large percentage of people without vehicles could well continue to grow.

Creating A More Secure and Safer City

The paradigm shift in planning "future cities" requires sophisticated use of technology to create a range of new capabilities. Efforts to create a "smarter" or more "intelligent" city cannot succeed piecemeal. Redesigning the information infrastructure of a city and making it responsive to the need of its populace will only succeed if it is truly designed and built on the needs of its citizens and proves in practice to be responsive to their needs. To further this effort, we must have holistic enterprises enabled by technology management tools that can quickly and nimbly enact emergency responses and trigger coordinated regional responses within a wide range of governmental jurisdictions and first responders. We can move forward through the effective use of advanced broadband information systems. This can allow us to become more energy efficient. It can also extend the number of people who are telecommuting at least a part of the time and decentralize many efforts that do not have to be geographically centralized in economies that are increasingly "service" oriented. In the age of the future city, enterprise management systems will necessarily become more important. This will be particularly true in terms of detecting potential emergency conditions and responding in a coordinated way across multiple jurisdictions. Fortunately a range of new IP based technologies and new management processes can indeed help cities to become more energy efficient, more prosperous, more responsive to its citizens, and provide enhanced safety and security. The above discussion is certainly not exhaustive of all the means that are evolving to make future cities safer and more secure. It is hoped, however, that some of the most important possibilities have been discussed.

Selected Bibliography

Joseph N. Pelton and Christine Robinson, "Seeing the Future Through the Lens of TeleGeography: Looking At New Ways to Address Global Warming, Clean Energy and the 9/11 Attacks", Editor, Cynthia Wagner, *Seeing the Future Through New Eyes*, (2008) World Future Society, Bethesda, MD.

Jane A. Bullock and George D. Haddow, "A New Model for Hazard Mitigation and Long Term Recovery Planning, in 2008-2009 *Disaster Resource Guide*, (2008) www.disaster-resource.com pp. 52-56.

CHAPTER 5

Conclusion

The development of new systems to make the city of the future more functional, more livable, and more sustainable can lead to the design of new cities and the re-invention of existing ones in remarkably different ways. There is no magic bullet or one single technology that will make one city significantly better than the rest.

The city with the most technology, the most expensive throughput equipment, and the most petabytes of storage does not necessarily "win". In fact, a city that overdoes on shiny new equipment that has not focused on its human needs and sustainability will almost certainly fail.

Human Needs

The successful attempt to plan for and implement the future city must—absolutely must—start with identifying ways to help the citizens and businesspeople that live in a community. This means finding ways to help this constituency become healthier, live longer, earn a better living, become more energy independent, and also be safer and more secure.

The planning for the future will not succeed if human needs are not at the forefront. Job Number One is to provide citizens with confidence that their longer-term community will be stronger economically, socially, artistically and politically. Planning and implementation must produce a future city that is ultimately able to meet all types of challenges from climate change to natural catastrophes, from technological shifts in employment to new needs in health care or educational services.

Evolutionary Planning and Implementation

The Smart City or Intelligent Community is not accomplished overnight. In fact the future is a moving target that requires constant adjustment to the real world. One can move to IP architecture or upgrade a transportation system to make it safer, more fuel efficient, less polluting or more responsive to citizen needs, but never will the upgrades be entirely finished.

Planning for the Smart City, as explained in Chapter 3, is a never-ending process that is best achieved if there are clear long-term goals and implementation plans that, on one hand, are geared to achieve the ultimate goals, but on the other hand, adaptable to shifts in budgetary needs, new technologies, or changes in the electorate's primary needs.

Prioritization

Another key point from Chapter 3 is that devising a plan that leverages the opportunities of "low hanging fruit" and giving emphasis to programs that can quickly provide useful return at low cost is a very sensible way to proceed. Must-have programs that give early payoffs need to be a clear-cut part of the planning methodology.

The city of Dundee, Scotland, made the investment in the Discovery Card, extending it to all of its citizen-benefit programs, which had very little incremental cost but lots of shorter term payoffs. The programs for training new nurses in Kenya were largely fixed and so they geared the program not for a few hundred but 22,000 trainees. The problem with priorization is, of course, teamwork. Everyone in the planning process must have an "All for One, and One for All" attitude to allow the prioritization effort to gain maximum effect and efficiency.

Security Is More Than Trying to Build A Wall to Keep Terrorists At Bay

The traditional concept of security has been to build a protective wall or a moat to shield oneself from invaders or attackers. In a world where transportation, energy and utility systems are controlled by computers, attacks can come from missiles, aircraft or laser beams, and valuable assets exist as digital bits of data, such traditional forms of security can be increasingly passé. A whole new approach to security must be developed. This new approach to security would pursue new concepts such as: (i) electronic distribution of critical functions; (ii) greater reliance on telework and movement of ideas rather things and people; (iii) implementation of new encryption systems that are superior to PKI public keyed infrastructure; and (iv) a host of other innovative approaches that go beyond screening people at airport inspection posts.

The Primacy of Sustainability

The longer-term planning for Intelligent Communities must look beyond greater efficiency of operation, integrated systems, and improved and more flexible services. Cities that today consume large quantities of non-renewable energy, generate carbon-based gases from transportation systems and contribute to climate change in a variety of ways cannot continue along the patterns established in the 19th and 20th century. New renewable energy sources, clean transportation systems, telecommuting and more are needed to combat global warming and reduce noxious gases and pollution of our water sources and oceans.

New Ways to Look to the Future

The creation of the future city implies a whole new and more positive way of contemplating an improved and more secure world. The result is not only a place but a society that is greener, with more energy independence, with improved transportation systems, with more creative and meaningful jobs, with better and more broadband communications and entertainment systems, and with enhanced education, training and health care systems. A perfect world will never be achieved. Nevertheless, a mindset that says "seek a better and more user responsive" city driven by a clear and viable economic plan can accomplish a great deal.

The World's Greatest Inventions

A

Agriculture, Forestry and Modern Systems of Cultivation and Crop Management

Airplanes, Helicopters, Jet Airplanes, Supersonic Transport, Space Planes, Unattended Autonomous Vehicles or High Altitude Platform Systems (UAVs-HAPS)

Airports. Train & Bus Terminals All Linked to Mass Transit Systems

Anatomy and Taxonomy—Understanding of Human Body and the Brain,

Antibiotics and Modern Medicines and Vaccines

Art, Statuary, Painting, Etchings, Mobiles, Crafts,

Artificial Intelligence and Expert Systems

Astrophysics, Astronomy, Structure and Form of Universe (Galaxies, Black Holes, Main Sequence of Stars, Planets and Moons, Quasars, Pulsars and Celestial Physics)

Atomic Energy-- Nuclear Fission and Fusion

Automobile, Trucks, Vans, Taxis, Rental Cars, Buses, Bull dozers, Backhoes, Cranes

B

Balloons and Atmospheric Sciences

Batteries, Fuel Cells, and Energy storage systems

Biology—Clear and Scientific Classification of Flora and Fauna

Birth Control, Reproductive Functions and Evolutionary Processes

Books, Encyclopedia, Dictionaries, Writing, Language, Paper, Newspapers, Magazines and Journals

The Brain, psycho-therapy, mental health treatment

Building structures and Materials, Bridges, Scaffolding, Civil Engineering, Elevators, and Escalators (See Heating, Ventilation, Air Conditioning)

C

Canals, Waterways, Pipelines, Aqueducts,

Candy, Pies, Cakes, Tarts and Desserts

Cellular Structure, genetics and modern biological systems

Chemical Engineering, Batteries, Combustion, and Chemical Energy

City and Towns and related infrastructure

Civil Engineering and Dynamics and Statics

Clothes, Costumes, Underwear, Lingerie, Clothing Materials and Clothing Designers

Competition, Innovation, and "Creative Destruction" (Truth is the Daughter of Time)

Communications & Remote Sensing Satellites plus other Applications Satellites for Weather, Geodetics, etc.

Computer Science and Processing, Software Development and Engineering, Neural Networks, Open and Proprietary Software, and Boolean Algebra

Cybernetic Organisms and Smart Machines

D

Dams, Levees, Tidal Basins, Flood Control, and Hydro-Electric Generators and Electric Power and RF Transmission Systems

DNA, RNA and Genetic Research & Engineering—Cloning

Disease Diagnosis and Pathology

Design (Industrial Design, Architecture, Product Design and Marketing Materials)

Dichotomy, Syllogisms, Logic Systems, Heuristic Models, Induction, Reduction, Deduction

E

Economics and Optimization Systems, Accounting Systems, Modern Management Techniques (See Design)

Education, Schools, Colleges and Universities, Tele-Education, Training, Self-Learning Computer Programs and Robots

Electric Motors

Electric Power Distribution System and Electric Grids

Electro-Magnetic Forces and Power and Storage Systems

Electronic Computer

Electronic and molecular memory systems

Empathy

Energy, Conservation of Energy, Renewable Energy (e.g. solar, wind, water and ocean mills, hydro-electric and tidal power, geothermal, photosynthesis, OTEC, Hydrogen, Fuel Cell, etc.)

Environmental Sciences, Ozone Layer, La Nina and El Nino, Detection of Global Warming

Esthetics (Human versus "Natural")

Evolution and biological processes of survival of the fittest and environmental adaptation

Eyeglasses, Disposable Lens, Lasik Surgery, Infrared night vision

F

Financial Processes, Stock Ownership, Bonds, Borrowing, Interest, & Free Markets

Fiber Optic Cable

Fiction, Novel, Plays, Science Fiction, Short Stories, Imagination

Fire and the control of fire for useful purposes from baking to smelting metals

Fishing, Hydroponics, Hydro-farming,

Foodstuffs, Frozen Food and Canned Goods, Seasoning and Preservation

Free Press and Free Political Process of Debate and Discovery

Fundamental Forces of the Universe—Gravity (Gravitons), Electro-Magnetic Force (Photons), Strong Nuclear Force (Gluons) and Weak Nuclear Force

G

Geology, Geodetics, Seismology and Vulcanology

Germs, Pathogens, and Antiseptics and Anesthesia

Government, Separation of Legislative, Executive and Judicial Branches, Role of the Fourth Estate

Guns, Catapults, Cannons, Mortars, Rail guns, and Weapons

H

Health Sciences, Dietary Research, Vitamins

Heating, Air Conditioning, HVAC, Air Filters and Humidifiers

Hot dog and Hamburger and Sandwiches

Housing and Hotels

Hydro Carbon Fuels, Petroleum Based materials, and Plastics

I

Indoor Plumbing, Water Towers and Pressure, Baths, Showers, Sewers, Hygiene, & Cleanliness

Internal Combustion Engine

Internet, E-Mail, the web, E-Commerce, Multi-Media, HTML, and Information Technology

International Treaties, International Relations, International Organizations, Visas, Immigration

Irrigation, Soil Nutrients, Tier and Contour Farming, Fertilization, Rotation Crops, and "Smart Farming" (See Agriculture)

J

Jellies, Jams, Honey, Sugar, and Artificial Sweeteners,

Judicial Process-Judicial Review and Appeals & Criminal and Penal Systems

K

Kilns, Ovens, Oasts, Bricks, and Ceramics

Kelp, Algae and other Sea Based Farming Systems

L

Language, Sign Language, Codes, Information Security and Privacy

Lasers and Masers

Law, Judicial Systems, Constitutional Rights, Appeal Systems,

Logical Systems-Induction, Deduction, Fuzzy Thinking,

Libraries

Lumber, Timber, Plywood, Nails, Tongue and Groove Construction, Shelters (See Building Structures)

M

Marriage, Core Families, Inheritance

Mathematics-Arithmetic, Algebra, Calculus, Geometry, Logical Systems, Trigonometry, Stochastic and Probability Processes, Differential Equations, Non-Linear Math and Fuzzy Thinking.

Metaphysics and Ethics

Meteorology and Modern Weather Forecasting Techniques

Molecular Engineering

Movies, Motion Picture, VCR, DVD and Amusement Parks

Multi-National Corporations, International Trade in Goods and Services, and Tariffs.

N

Nation State

Navigational Systems, Compasses, Radar, Sonar

Numbering Systems, Base 10, Base 2, Pi, Natural Logarithmic "e", Fibonacci Numbers

O

Optics, Visible Light, Ultra-violet, Infra-Red Energy, Holograms,

Ozone Layer, Solar Storms and Sunspots, and Radiation Shielding

P

Perspective and Proportion

Photography, Video Cameras and Multi-Media

Physics- Fundamental Laws, Gravity, Electro-Magnetism and Weak & Strong Nuclear Forces, Sub-Atomic Particles, Relativity, and Time-Space Continuum

Plastics and other New Materials Derived from Petrochemicals or other Chemical Substances

Political Process, Representational Democracy, Checks and Balances, Political Polling, Taxes and Tariffs

Printing Press

Prosthetics and Speech Therapy and Restorative Surgery

R

Radio and Radio Communications Devices

Renaissance Thinking and Integrated Systems

Risk, Insurance, Probability and Statistics (See Mathemathics)

Roads and Highways and Freeways

Robotic devices

Rocket Ships

S

Sanitation and Trash Removal Systems

Scientific Method -Induction, Deduction, R&D and Testing of Hypotheses (See Dichotomy)

Semi-conductors, Transistors, VLSI, Monolithic Devices, MEMS, silicon, gallium arsenide and other semi-conductors

Sexual Freedom and Equality of the Sexes

Ships, Arks, Boats, Yachts, Barges, Catamarans, Tankers and Carriers (Steam, Sail and Motor Driven) as well as port and port systems with cranes and docks

Sliced Bread, Packaged Food, and Nutritional Requirements

Sociology and Psychology

Space Exploration and Applications (See Astrophysics and Communications Satellites)

Steel, Iron, Copper, Aluminum, Rebar, Alloys, Carbon Epoxy Materials, Bucky Balls, Re-Enforced Concrete,

Ceramic Tiles, Plastics, Other Building and Product Materials

Sterilization, Antiseptics and Anti-biotic Ointments

Superconductivity and Josephson Junctions

Surgery and Modern Medical Practices

T

Telephone and Telephone Numbering, Switching and Signaling Systems and Telegraph, Telex and Fax through IP Based Telecommunications Systems

Telescope and Microscope

Television and High Definition Television

Tools and Machines (Wheels, Screws, Pumps, Hobs, Lathes, Pulleys, Winches, Vices, Levers, Drills, Plows, Cantilevers, etc.)

Trains and Railroad Systems

Transistor, VLSI, monolithic devices, MEMS, and Nano-technology

Transportation systems, especially mass transportation and clean energy transport systems

U

Umbrellas, Coats, Thermal Underwear, Goggles, Kevlar, Bullet Proof Clothing

Universities and colleges, professional training, research institutes, laboratories

V

Videoconferencing and Tele-commuting

Vitamins and Nutritional Sciences

Values of Humanity, Empathy and Caring

W

War, Humane Practices of, Geneva Convention, War Crimes

Water Treatment and Purifications Systems (See Canals)

Writing Instruments, Pens, Pencils, Chalk, Crayons, Markers, Erasable Boards (See Books)

XYZ

X-Ray and MRIs

Yoyos and Toys

Zoos and Botanical Gardens

Glossary of Terms

Broadband: data transmission where multiple pieces of data are sent simultaneously to increase the effective rate of transmission, regardless of actual data rate. Sometimes referred to as a high-speed Internet, broadband is an 'always on' fast connection to the Internet.

Byte: This is a unit of computer storage or memory and consists of 8 bits digital information and considered more or less equal to one word.

Call Center: A customer contact function that fields incoming service and help requests and may conduct outgoing marketing and telemarketing activities.

Citizen Relationship System: refers to collaborative enterprise processes and technologies that support customer interactions throughout all channels.

Data Center: A secure location for web hosting servers. Data centers are designed to assure that the computers and servers and the data housed on them are protected from environmental hazards and security breaches.

DOD: U.S. Department of Defense

DOE: U.S. Department of Energy

Enterprise Infrastructure (EI): Systems and technology for information management

EPA: Environmental Protection Agency of the United States

FEMA: Federal Emergency Management Organization of the United States

First Responders: Security, aid-providing and service restoration personnel. These include police, fire-fighters, Emergency Medical Treatment (EMT), 911 operators and those involved in restoring key utilities such as telecommunications, gas, electricity, water and sewage. Geographic Information System (GIS): an information system for capturing, storing, analyzing, managing and presenting data which is spatially referenced (linked to location).

HALE: High Altitude Long Endurance platforms that can be used for communications, broadcasting, surveillance, and earth observation purposes

HAPS: High Altitude Platform Systems. This is another term, designated by the ITU, to describe a HALE.

IETF: Internet Engineering Task Force. This is the group that approves standards for the Internet.

Internet City: one that uses universal IP architecture in provision of all electronic and information services. (See also Smart City)

Internet Protocol (IP): the rules and encoding specifications for sending data; the method by which data is sent from one computer to another over the Internet.

Information Technology (IT): A reference often used for the computer based networking industry.

IPC3: refers to technology and modern communication architectures which integrate existing and evolving city technology infrastructure and applications into future Smart City platform to increase efficiency and cost-effective. This is a unique solution developed by the Bearing Point Corporation, but a similar generic solution would be applied by other urban planners with expertise in broadband networking systems.

IR: Infra-Red communications systems

ITU: The International Telecommunication Union, the United Nations specialized international organizations that devises standards for telecommunications and broadcasting around the world.

Negroponte Flip: This is a reference to an idea propounded by Nicholas Negroponte of the MIT Media Lab in the late 1990s that broadband services would migrate to "wire" or fiber optic cable because of limited radio frequency capacity to accommodate broadband services and that narrowband telephone and texting services would all migrate to wireless systems. In fact both narrowband and broadband services are today offered by an integrated mix of wire and wireless media. (See Pelton Merge)

Network Operations Center (NOC): a physical place where communications networks are monitored, administrated and maintained.

NGOs: Non-Governmental Organizations. There are many such organizations such as the Red Cross, the Red

Crescent and Care International that provide emergency and disaster relief.

NRC: Nuclear Regulatory Commission

OECD: Organization of Economic Cooperation and Development. These twenty plus nations represent the most economically developed countries in the world.

Pelton Merge: The idea that IT planners should consider the integrated provision of broadband services over a flexible and multi-media based IT network that would include all forms of "wire" and "wireless communications. Rather than having urban planners relying exclusively on fiber optics for broadband, the Pelton Merge, would create software—largely IP based—to allow the networks to include fiber, coax, terrestrial RF wireless, infrared, satellites, high altitude long endurance (HALE), and powerline communications. This approach provides for a more flexible backup of service, promotes intermedia cost competition, and allows much greater mobility to customers. (See Negroponte Flip)

Performance Architecture: a framework to measure the performance of initiatives and their contribution to program performance.

Petabyte: A quadrillion bytes, which can also be expressed as 1,000,000,000,000,000 bytes

PLC: Power line communications

RF: Radio Frequency

RFID: Radio Frequency Identification

Security (Firewall, DMZ, VPN): methods used to protect data from unauthorized access (eg, encryption).

Service Architecture: provides a common framework and vocabulary to characterize the technology and business components that collectively comprise business and technology infrastructure.

SLA: Service Level Agreements

Smart City Ecosystem (SCE): defines the critical role of information and communication systems in depicting interrelations between people, process and technology.

Smart City: a city built around new broadband IT infrastructure, but also embracing other "intelligent" concepts that ultimately delivers enhanced public services, green cities and better environmental management, business and job growth, expanded foreign investment and public safety. This type of highly capable urban development is also referred to as an Intelligent Community or future city

SMART: an acronym that includes the following key elements needed to plan and implement a Smart City program: (S)pecific objectives and components, (M)easurable results, (A)greed to by all stakeholders, (R)ealistic, and (T)ime framed by the project's deadlines.

SNP: Special Needs Population. Those parties that need special assistance during emergency conditions.

Technical Architecture: provides a foundation to describe the standards, specifications and technologies supporting the delivery, exchange and construction of business service or service components of each of the new business or service solution.

Terabyte: This is 1 trillion bytes, which can also be expressed as 1,000,000,000,000 bytes

USDA: United States Department of Agriculture

Index